Taking An ASE Certification Test

This study guide will help prepare you to take and pass the ASE test. It contains descriptions of the types of questions used on the test, the task list from which the test questions are derived, a review of the task list subject information, and a practice test containing ASE style questions.

ABOUT ASE

The National Institute for Automotive Service Excellence (ASE) is a non-profit organization founded in 1972 for the purpose of improving the quality of automotive service and repair through the voluntary testing and certification of automotive technicians. Currently, there are over 400,000 professional technicians certified by ASE in over 40 different specialist areas.

ASE certification recognizes your knowledge and experience, and since it is voluntary, taking and passing an ASE certification test also demonstrates to employers and customers your commitment to your profession. It can mean better compensation and increased employment opportunities as well.

ASE not only certifies technician competency, it also promotes the benefits of technician certification to the motoring public. Repair shops that employ at least one ASE technician can display the ASE sign. Establishments where 75 percent of technicians are certified, with at least one technician certified in each area of service offered by the business, are eligible for the ASE Blue Seal of Excellence program. ASE encourages consumers to patronize these shops through media campaigns and car care clinics.

To become ASE certified, you must pass at least one ASE exam and have at least two years of related work experience. Technicians that pass specified tests in a series earn Master Technician status.

Your certification is valid for five years, after which time you must retest to retain certification, demonstrating that you have kept up with the changing technology in the field.

THE ASE TEST

An ASE test consists of forty to eighty multiple-choice questions. Test questions are written by a panel of technical experts from vehicle, parts and equipment manufacturers, as well as working technicians and technical education instructors. All questions have been pre-tested and quality checked on a national sample of technicians. The questions are derived from information presented in the task list, which details the knowledge that a technician must have to pass an ASE test and be recognized as competent in that category. The task list is periodically updated by ASE in response to changes in vehicle technology and repair techniques.

© Advanstar Communications Inc. 2012.3

Customer Service 1-800-240-1968
FAX 218-740-6437
e-mail: PassTheASE@advanstar.com
URL: www.PassTheASE.com

T6 - ELECTRICAL/ELECTRONIC SYSTEMS

Taking An ASE Certification Test

There are five types of questions on an ASE test:
- **Direct, or Completion**
- **MOST Likely**
- **Technician A and Technician B**
- **EXCEPT**
- **LEAST Likely**

Direct, or Completion

This type of question is the kind that is most familiar to anyone who has taken a multiple-choice test: you must answer a direct question or complete a statement with the correct answer. There are four choices given as potential answers, but only one is correct. Sometimes the correct answer to one of these questions is clear, however in other cases more than one answer may seem to be correct. In that case, read the question carefully and choose the answer that is most correct. Here is an example of this type of test question:

A compression test shows that one cylinder is too low. A leakage test on that cylinder shows that there is excessive leakage. During the test, air could be heard coming from the tailpipe. Which of the following could be the cause?
A. broken piston rings
B. bad head gasket
C. bad exhaust gasket
D. an exhaust valve not seating

There is only one correct answer to this question, answer D. If an exhaust valve is not seated, air will leak from the combustion chamber by way of the valve out to the tailpipe and make an audible sound. Answer C is wrong because an exhaust gasket has nothing to do with combustion chamber sealing. Answers A and B are wrong because broken rings or a bad head gasket would have air leaking through the oil filler or coolant system.

MOST Likely

This type of question is similar to a direct question but it can be more challenging because all or some of the answers may be nearly correct. However, only one answer is the most correct. For example:

When a cylinder head with an overhead camshaft is discovered to be warped, which of the following is the most correct repair option?
A. replace the head
B. check for cracks, straighten the head, surface the head
C. surface the head, then straighten it
D. straighten the head, surface the head, check for cracks

The most correct answer is B. It makes no sense to perform repairs on a cylinder head that might not be usable. The head should first be checked for warpage and cracks. Therefore, answer B is more correct than answer D. The head could certainly be replaced, but the cost factor may be prohibitive and availability may be limited, so answer B is more correct than answer A. If the top of the head is warped enough to interfere with cam bore alignment and/or restrict free movement of the camshaft, the head must be straightened before it is resurfaced, so answer C is wrong.

Technician A and Technician B

These questions are the kind most commonly associated with the ASE test. With these questions you are asked to choose which technician statement is correct, or whether they both are correct or incorrect. This type of question can be difficult because very often you may find one technician's statement to be clearly correct or incorrect while the other may not be so obvious. Do you choose one technician or both? The key to answering these questions is to carefully examine each technician's statement independently and judge it on its own merit. Here is an example of this type of question:

A vehicle equipped with rack-and-pinion steering is having the front end inspected. Technician A says that the inner tie rod ends should be inspected while in their normal running position. Technician B says that if movement is felt between the tie rod stud and the socket while the tire is moved in and out, the inner tie rod should be replaced. Who is correct?
A. Technician A
B. Technician B
C. Both A and B
D. Neither A or B

The correct answer is C; both technicians' statements are correct. Technician B is clearly correct because any play felt between the tie-rod stud and the socket while the tire is moved in and out indicates that the assembly is worn and requires replacement. However, Technician A is also correct because inner tie-rods should be inspected while in their normal running position, to prevent binding that may occur when the suspension is allowed to hang free.

EXCEPT

This kind of question is sometimes called a negative question because you are asked to give the incorrect answer. All of the possible answers given are correct EXCEPT one. In effect, the correct answer to the question is the one that is wrong. The word EXCEPT is always capitalized in these questions. For example:

All of the following are true of torsion bars **EXCEPT**:
A. They can be mounted longitudinally or transversely.
B. They serve the same function as coil springs.

C. They are interchangeable from side-to-side
D. They can be used to adjust vehicle ride height.

The correct answer is C. Torsion bars are not normally interchangeable from side-to-side. This is because the direction of the twisting or torsion is not the same on the left and right sides. All of the other answers contain true statements regarding torsion bars.

LEAST Likely

This type of question is similar to EXCEPT in that once again you are asked to give the answer that is wrong. For example:

Blue-gray smoke comes from the exhaust of a vehicle during deceleration. Of the following, which cause is **LEAST** likely?
A. worn valve guides
B. broken valve seals
C. worn piston rings
D. clogged oil return passages

The correct answer is C. Worn piston rings will usually make an engine smoke worse under acceleration. All of the other causes can allow oil to be drawn through the valve guides under the high intake vacuum that occurs during deceleration.

PREPARING FOR THE ASE TEST

Begin preparing for the test by reading the task list. The task list describes the actual work performed by a technician in a particular specialty area. Each question on an ASE test is derived from a task or set of tasks in the list. Familiarizing yourself with the task list will help you to concentrate on the areas where you need to study.

The text section of this study guide contains information pertaining to each of the tasks in the task list. Reviewing this information will prepare you to take the practice test.

Take the practice test and compare your answers with the correct answer explanations. If you get an answer wrong and don't understand why, go back and read the information pertaining to that question in the text.

After reviewing the tasks and the subject information and taking the practice test, you should be prepared to take the ASE test or be aware of areas where further study is needed. When studying with this study guide or any other source of information, use the following guidelines to make sure the time spent is as productive as possible:

- Concentrate on the subject areas where you are weakest.
- Arrange your schedule to allow specific times for studying.
- Study in an area where you will not be distracted.
- Don't try to study after a full meal or when you are tired.
- Don't wait until the last minute and try to 'cram' for the test.

REGISTERING FOR ASE COMPUTER-BASED TESTING

Registration for the ASE CBT tests can be done online in myASE or over the phone. While not mandatory, it is recommended that you establish a myASE account on the ASE website (www.ase.com). This can be a big help in managing the ASE certification process, as your test scores and certification expiry dates are all listed there.

Test times are available during two-month windows with a one-month break in between. This means that there is a total of eight months over the period of the calendar year that ASE testing is available.

Testing can be scheduled during the daytime, night, and weekends for maximum flexibility. Also, results are available immediately after test completion. Printed certificates are mailed at the end of the two-month test window. If you fail a test, you will not be allowed to register for the same test until the next two-month test window.

TAKING THE ASE TEST – COMPUTER-BASED TESTING (CBT)

On test day, bring some form of photo identification with you and be sure to arrive at the test center 30 minutes early to give sufficient time to check in. Once you have checked in, the test supervisor will issue you some scratch paper and pencils, as well as a composite vehicle test booklet if you are taking advanced tests. You will then be seated at a computer station and given a short online tutorial on how to complete the ASE CBT tests. You may skip the tutorial if you are already familiar with the CBT process.

The test question format is similar to those found in written ASE tests. Regular certification tests have a time limit of 1 to 2 hours, depending on the test. Recertification tests are 30 to 45 minutes, and the L1 and L2 advanced level tests are capped at 2 hours. The time remaining for your test is displayed on the top left of the test window. You are given a warning when you have 5 minutes left to complete the test.

Read through each question carefully. If you don't know the answer to a question and need to think about it, click on the "Flag" button and move on to the next question. You may also go back to previous questions by pressing the "Previous Question" button. Don't spend too much time on any one question. After you have worked through to the end of the test, check your remaining time and go

Taking An ASE Certification Test

back and answer the questions you flagged. Very often, information found in questions later in the test can help answer some of the ones with which you had difficulty.

Some questions may have more content than what can fit on one screen. If this is the case, there will be a "More" button displayed where the "Next Question" button would ordinarily appear. A scrolling bar will also appear, showing what part of the question you are currently viewing. Once you have viewed all of the related content for the question, the "Next Question" button will reappear.

You can change answers on any of the questions before submitting the test for scoring. At the end of the examination, you will be shown a table with all of the question numbers. This table will show which questions are answered, which are unanswered, and which have been flagged for review. You will be given the option to review all the questions, review the flagged questions, or review the unanswered questions from this page. This table can be reviewed at any time during the exam by clicking the "Review" button.

If you are running out of time and still have unanswered test questions, guess the answers if necessary to make sure every question is answered. Do not leave any answers blank. It is to your advantage to answer every question, because your test score is based on the number of correct answers. A guessed answer could be correct, but a blank answer can never be.

Once you are satisfied that all of the questions are complete and ready for scoring, click the "Submit for Scoring" button. If you are scheduled for more than one test, the next test will begin immediately. If you are done with testing, you will be asked to complete a short survey regarding the CBT test experience. As you are leaving the test center, your supervisor will give you a copy of your test results. Your scores will also be available on myASE within two business days.

To learn exactly where and when the ASE Certification Tests are available in your area, as well as the costs involved in becoming ASE certified, please contact ASE directly for registration information.

The National Institute for Automotive Service Excellence
101 Blue Seal Drive, S.E. Suite 101
Leesburg, VA 20175
1-800-390-6789
http://www.ase.com

Table of Contents
T6 - Electrical/Electronic Systems

Test Specifications And Task List 6

General Electrical System Diagnosis. 9

Battery & Starting System Diagnosis And Repair 21

Charging System Diagnosis And Repair 31

Lighting Systems Diagnosis And Repair 38

Related Vehicle Systems Diagnosis And Repair. 47

Sample Test Questions 64

Answers To Study-Guide Test Questions 72

Glossary 77

Advanstar endeavors to collect and include complete, correct and current information in this publication but does not warrant that any or all of such information is complete, correct or current. Publisher does not assume, and hereby disclaims, any liability to any person or entity for any loss or damage caused by errors or omissions of any kind, whether resulting from negligence, accident or any other cause. If you do notice any error, we would appreciate if you would bring such error to our attention.

Test Specifications And Task List

Medium/Heavy Electrical/Electronic Systems

TEST SPECIFICATIONS FOR MEDIUM/HEAVY
ELECTRICAL/ELECTRONIC SYSTEMS
(TEST T6)

CONTENT AREA	NUMBER OF QUESTIONS IN ASE TEST	PERCENTAGE OF COVERAGE IN ASE TEST
A. General Electrical System Diagnosis	14	28%
B. Battery and Starting System Diagnosis and Repair	11	22%
C. Charging System Diagnosis and Repair	7	14%
D. Lighting Systems Diagnosis and Repair	6	12%
E. Related Vehicle Systems Diagnosis and Repair	12	24%
Total	50	100%

The 5-year Recertification Test will cover the same content areas as those listed above. However, the number of questions in each content area of the Recertification Test will be reduced by about one-half.

The following pages list the tasks covered in each content area. These task descriptions offer detailed information to technicians preparing for the test and persons who may be instructing Medium/Heavy Electrical/ Electronic Systems technicians. The task list may also serve as a guideline for question writers, reviewers and test assemblers.

It should be noted that the number of questions in each content area may not equal the number of tasks listed. Some of the tasks are complex and broad in scope and may be covered by several questions. Other tasks are simple and narrow in scope, and one question may cover several tasks. The main purpose for listing the tasks is to describe accurately what is done on the job, not to make each task correspond to a particular test question.

MEDIUM/HEAVY ELECTRICAL/ELECTRONIC SYSTEMS TASK LIST

A. GENERAL ELECTRICAL SYSTEMS DIAGNOSIS
(14 questions)

Task 1 – Check applied voltages, circuit voltages, and voltage drops in electrical/electronic circuits using digital multimeter (DMM), or appropriate test equipment.

Task 2 – Check current flow in electrical/electronic circuits and components using a digital multimeter (DMM), clamp-on ammeter, or appropriate test equipment.

Task 3 – Check continuity and resistance in electrical/electronic circuits and components using a digital multimeter (DMM), or appropriate test equipment.

Task 4 – Find shorts, grounds, and opens in electrical/electronic circuits.

Task 5 – Diagnose key-off battery drain (parasitic draw) problems; determine needed repairs.

Task 6 – Inspect and test fusible links, circuit breakers, fuses, and other circuit protection devices; including reset when required.

Task 7 – Inspect and test spike suppression diodes/resistors and capacitors.

Task 8 – Inspect and test relays and solenoids (including solid state devices).

Task 9 – Read, interpret electrical schematic diagrams and symbols.

Task 10 – Diagnose failures in the data communications bus network; determine needed repairs.

Task 11 – Diagnose vehicle electronic control systems using appropriate diagnostic tools, software, and service information; check and record diagnostic codes; determine needed repairs.

Task 12 – Connect diagnostic tool to vehicle; access and verify parameters and calibration settings; perform updates as needed.

B. BATTERY & STARTING SYSTEM DIAGNOSIS AND REPAIR (11 questions)

Task 1 – Determine battery state of

Test Specifications And Task List

charge by measuring terminal post voltage using a digital multimeter (DMM).

Task 2 – Perform battery tests (load and capacitance); determine needed service.

Task 3 – Inspect, clean, service, or replace battery, cables, and terminal connections.

Task 4 – Inspect, clean, repair or replace battery boxes, mounts, and hold downs.

Task 5 – Charge battery using appropriate method for battery type.

Task 6 – Jump start a vehicle using jumper cables and a booster battery or appropriate auxiliary power supply.

Task 7 – Diagnose low voltage disconnect (LVD) systems; determine needed repairs.

Task 8 – Test/monitor battery and starting system voltage during cranking; determine needed repairs.

Task 9 – Perform starting circuit voltage drop tests; determine needed repairs.

Task 10 – Inspect, test, and replace starter control circuit switches, relays, connectors, terminals and wires (including thermal over crank protection).

Task 11 – Diagnose starter cranking inhibit systems; determine needed repairs.

Task 12 – Inspect, test, and replace starter relays and solenoids/switches including integrated MAG switch (IMS).

Task 13 – Inspect, clean, repair, or replace cranking circuit cables, connectors, and terminals.

Task 14 – Remove and replace starter; inspect flywheel ring gear or flex plate.

Task 15 – Differentiate between electrical and/or mechanical problems that cause a slow crank, no crank, extended cranking, or a cranking noise condition.

C. CHARGING SYSTEM DIAGNOSIS AND REPAIR
(7 questions)

Task 1 – Verify operation of charging system circuit monitors; determine needed repairs.

Task 2 – Diagnose the cause of a no-charge, low-charge or overcharge condition; determine needed repairs.

Task 3 – Inspect, adjust and replace alternator drive belts/gears, pulleys, fans, mounting brackets and tensioners.

Task 4 – Perform charging system voltage (AC and DC) and amperage output tests; determine needed repairs.

Task 5 – Perform charging circuit voltage drop tests; determine needed repairs.

Task 6 – Remove and replace alternator.

Task 7 – Inspect, repair or replace connectors, terminals, and wires.

D. LIGHTING SYSTEMS DIAGNOSIS AND REPAIR
(6 questions)

Task 1 – Diagnose the cause of brighter-than-normal, intermittent, dim or no headlight and daytime running light (DRL) operation.

Task 2 – Test, replace, and aim headlights and auxiliary lights.

Task 3 – Inspect, test, repair, or replace headlight switches, dimmer switches, control components, relays, sockets, connectors, terminals, and wires.

Task 4 – Inspect, test, repair, or replace truck and trailer lighting circuit switches, bulbs, light-emitting diodes (LEDs), sockets, control components, relays, connectors, terminals, and wires.

Task 5 – Inspect, test, repair or replace dash light circuit switches, bulbs, LEDs, sockets, fiber optic cable, circuit boards, connectors, terminals, wires.

Task 6 – Inspect, test, repair or replace interior cab light circuit switches, bulbs, LEDs, sockets, connectors, terminals and wires.

Task 7 – Inspect, test, adjust, repair or replace stoplight circuit switches, relays, bulbs, LEDs, sockets, connectors, terminals, and wires.

Task 8 – Diagnose the cause of turn signal and hazard light system malfunctions; determine needed repairs.

Task 9 – Inspect, test, repair or replace turn signal and hazard circuit flashers or control components, switches, relays, bulbs, LEDs, sockets, connectors, terminals, and wires.

Task 10 – Inspect, test, adjust, repair or replace back-up light and warning devices, circuit switches, bulbs, LEDs, sockets, connectors, terminals and wires.

Task 11 – Inspect and test trailer light cord connector and cable; determine needed repairs.

E. RELATED VEHICLE SYSTEMS DIAGNOSIS AND REPAIR
(12 questions)

Task 1 – Diagnose the cause of intermittent, inaccurate, or no gauge readings; determine needed repairs.

Task 2 – Diagnose the cause of data bus driven gauge malfunctions; determine needed repairs.

Task 3 – Inspect, test, adjust, repair or replace gauge circuit sending units, sensors, gauges, connectors, terminals and wires.

Task 4 – Inspect, test, repair or replace warning devices (lights and audible) circuit sending units, sensors, circuit boards/control modules, bulbs, audible component, sockets, connectors, terminals, and wires.

Task 5 – Inspect, test and replace electronic speedometer, electronic instrumentation systems; verify proper calibration for vehicle application.

Task 6 – Diagnose the cause of constant, intermittent or no horn operation, determine needed repairs.

Task 7 – Inspect, test, repair or replace horn circuit relays, horns, switches, clock spring, connectors, terminals and wires.

Task 8 – Diagnose the cause of constant, intermittent or no wiper operation; diagnose the cause of wiper speed control and/or park problems; determine needed repairs.

Task 9 – Inspect, test, repair or

Training for Certification

Test Specifications And Task List

replace wiper motor and transmission mechanical linkage, arms and blades, relays, switches, connectors, terminals, and wires.

Task 10 – Inspect, test, repair or replace windshield washer motor or pump/relay assembly, switches, connectors, terminals and wires.

Task 11 – Inspect, test, repair or replace side view mirror motors, heater circuit grids, relays, switches, connectors, terminals and wires.

Task 12 – Inspect, test, repair or replace heater and A/C electrical components including: A/C clutches, motors, resistors, relays, switches, controls, connectors, terminals and wires.

Task 13 – Inspect, test, repair or replace cigarette lighter and/or auxiliary power outlet case, integral fuse, connectors, terminals and wires.

Task 14 – Diagnose the cause of slow, intermittent or no power window operation; determine needed repairs.

Task 15 – Inspect, test, repair and replace motors, switches, relays, connectors, terminals and wires.

Task 16 – Diagnose inverter/shore power systems; determine needed repairs.

Task 17 – Diagnose the cause of poor, intermittent or no operation of electric door locks; determine needed repairs.

Task 18 – Inspect test, repair, or replace electric door lock circuit switches, relays, controllers, actuators/solenoids, connectors, terminals, and wires.

Task 19 – Inspect, test, repair and replace cruise control electrical components.

Task 20 – Inspect, test, replace engine cooling fan electrical control components.

Task 21 – Inspect, test, and replace electric fuel supply/transfer pump control components.

The preceding Task List details all of the related informational subject matter you are expected to know in order to sit for this ASE Certification Test. Your own years of experience as a technician in the professional automotive service repair trade also should provide you with added background.

Finally, a conscientious review of the self-study material provided in this Training for ASE Certification unit also should help you to be adequately prepared to take this test.

General Electrical System Diagnosis

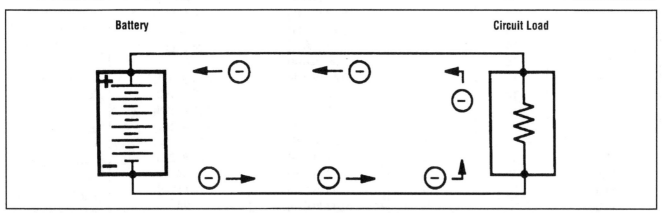

The actual direction of electron flow in a circuit. Current consists of the flow of electrons. Since electrons have a negative charge, and since like charges repel, they are repelled by the battery negative terminal and attracted to the battery positive terminal. *(Courtesy: Interstate Battery System of America)*

ELECTRICITY BASICS

For electrons to move or flow, they need a path along which to travel. This path is called a circuit, and it starts at a source, which we usually think of as positive. It ends at what we call negative, or ground. This path is necessary so that every atom in the circuit can continuously receive an electron to replace each one it has given up as the current flows.

Metal passages or conductors carry electrons through automotive circuits. Wires are the most common conductors. Wires lead electrons to and through loads. Loads are devices that offer resistance to current flow and in so doing they allow electrons do useful work.

A complete circuit is necessary if electricity is to flow. A circuit represents a power supply such as a battery or generator, a load, such as a motor, gauge, resistor, or light, and two conductors. One, the 'hot wire,' carries the current from the positive terminal of the battery or generator output terminal to the load using electrical voltage, or pressure.

The other, the "ground wire," carries the current back to the power supply. The ground circuit may consist of either wiring specifically intended for that purpose, un-insulated straps, or the metal body or frame of the vehicle itself.

All four parts of the circuit must be present, or electrical current will not flow.

The actual direction the current flows is from ground, or the negative side of a circuit or battery toward the positive side. This occurs because electrons, which make up current, have a negative charge, just as the battery negative terminal does. Thus, the positive terminal of a battery actually draws the electrons toward it. In spite of this fact, it is much simpler to think of the positive side of the circuit as the source of the pressure, which makes the current flow from there to the negative side.

To control the flow of electrons, switches are installed along the circuit path. A switch stops the flow of electricity by opening its contacts (points at which one conductor meets another), and interrupting the current path.

Another control device found in a circuit is a fuse or circuit breaker.

A fuse is an electrical safety component, consisting of a piece of metal with a low melting point.

When the current flow becomes too great for a circuit's wiring to handle, resistance to flow increases, and so does heat. Soon, the metal inside the fuse melts, and interrupts the flow of electricity. When properly sized, a fuse will interrupt the flow in a circuit long before the temperature of the wiring or any switch or other component has reached a temperature that is too high. Once the metal in a fuse has melted, the fuse must be replaced.

A circuit breaker does the same job as a fuse, but instead of using a piece of metal that melts, it uses contacts that open to interrupt the circuit.

The two most common types of circuit breakers are called thermal and magnetic. Thermal circuit breakers work by reaction to heat. Internally, a bimetal connects the two circuit breaker contacts. As heat increases due to excessive current flow in the circuit, the bimetal strip moves away from one of the internal contacts, interrupting current flow. Thermal circuit breakers cannot

General Electrical System Diagnosis

Metric Size mm2	SAE Gauge	Multiple Strand Number Of Strands	Multiple Strand Strand Diameter mm (Inch)	Strand Diameter mm (Inch)
0.5	20	7	0.31 (0.012)	0.81 (0.032)
0.8	18	7	0.38 (0.015)	1.02 (0.040)
0.8	18	19	0.23 (0.009)	NA
1.0	16	7	0.46 (0.018)	1.30 (0.051)
1.0	16	19	0.28 (0.011)	NA
2.0	14	7	0.59 (0.023)	1.63 (0.064)
2.0	14	19	0.36 (0.014)	NA
3.0	12	19	0.45 (0.018)	2.06 (0.081)
5.0	10	19	0.57 (0.022)	2.59 (0.102)
8.0	8	19	0.71 (0.028)	3.29 (0.129)
13.0	6	37	0.66 (0.026)	4.11 (0.162)
19.0	4	61	0.63 (0.025)	5.18 (0.204)
32.0	2	127	0.57 (0.022)	6.55 (0.258)
32.0	2	133	0.57 (0.022)	NA
40.0	1	127	0.63 (0.025)	7.34 (0.289)
40.0	1	133	0.63 (0.025)	NA
50.0	0	127	0.71 (0.028)	8.25 (0.325)
50.0	0	133	0.71 (0.028)	NA
62.0	00	127	0.79 (0.033)	9.27 (0.365)
62.0	00	133	0.79 (0.033)	NA
81.0	000	259	0.63 (0.025)	10.41 (0.410)
103.0	0000	259	0.71 (0.028)	11.68 (0.460)

Metric and SAE wire size information. It is important to use the proper wire size for the application. (Courtesy: Interstate Battery System of America)

be manually reset. They must cool down to allow the bimetal strip to return to its normal position, closing the circuit.

Magnetic circuit breakers use an electromagnet to trip the circuit breaker switch. As current exceeds a predetermined level, a magnetic field is created inside the circuit breaker. Magnetism draws the circuit breaker switch away from its internal contact, interrupting current flow. Unlike the thermal circuit breaker, the magnetic circuit breaker can be manually reset.

NOTE: *If excessive is present in the circuit, replacement fuses will also melt or the circuit breaker will continue to cycle. Simply replacing the fuse or resetting the circuit breaker will not correct the underlying cause of the problem.*

A major variable that affects resistance is wire diameter. Just as a large-diameter pipe allows more fluid to pass than a smaller-diameter pipe, a large-diameter wire allows more electrons to flow through it than a smaller-diameter wire.

For example, a starter needs more current to operate than a headlight, so its wiring is much larger than the headlight's. If we were to supply current to a starter with a thin, headlight wire, the wire would resist the larger flow of electrons, and heat would be generated. Voltage would also drop through the wire.

When properly sized, wires carry current (amps) at a pace that produces very little resistance and heat. A hot electrical wire means more electrons are trying to flow through it than the wire is capable of carrying. Usually this is a sign of trouble. Typically, that trouble would be either a deterioration of the wire, possibly due to a number of individual strands being broken in a conductor consisting of many individual strands, or higher-than-normal current flow, due to a problem in the wiring or the load.

Another variable that affects resistance is wire condition. Wire that is partially cut behaves much the same as if the entire length of wire were of a smaller diameter—like a kink in a fluid-carrying hose.

Yet another source of unwanted resistance is dirt or corrosion in connectors and switches. When a connection gets "dirty" or corrodes, portions of the metal conductors combine with oxygen to form non-metallic material that does not conduct electricity. The conductors get smaller as fresh metal is replaced by corroded material. The smaller conductors can inhibit electron flow to the point where a circuit will no longer operate.

In general, resistance anywhere in the wiring or in a wiring connector interferes with the operation of some part of the vehicle and carries with it, at least potentially, the byproduct of undesirable levels of heat. Such heat can easily start a fire.

Not all resistance is undesirable, however. Loads impose a certain amount of resistance as electrons are put to work, reducing voltage from something very near the 14 volts the alternator produces, down to nearly

General Electrical System Diagnosis

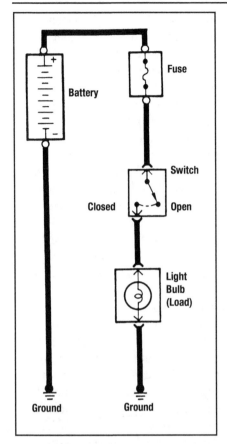

Simple light circuit.
(Courtesy: GM Corp.)

zero where a light, gauge, or motor is grounded. A primary difference is that this resistance produces light or useful work that does something for the vehicle's owner. If the resistance occurs elsewhere, however, as in a wire, connector, or ground, it will interfere with the function of some electrical component of the vehicle and produce an operating problem.

For example, inside a light bulb there is a short piece of high resistance wire called a filament. When current flows through the bulb, the resistance offered by the filament generates heat. In fact, the filament quickly becomes white-hot and the bulb glows. A blower motor offers resistance to current flow as its stator windings produce an intense magnetic field. In so doing, the motor spins a shaft and moves air.

So, there are two essential differences between the resistances generated by a bulb or motor and that produced by a frayed wire or corroded connector. The first is the bulb or motor produces useful work, the second is that resistance offered by a load is safe, while resistance offered by a wire or connector is potentially dangerous.

One byproduct of useful work is the removal of at least a portion of the energy from the scene, which helps prevent the accumulation of dangerous heat. Also, the light or motor is located where it can easily be cooled by surrounding air, to prevent the accumulation of dangerous levels of heat.

Contrast this with an electrical connector or wire. These items are often heavily insulated, or at least have heavily insulated components. Insulation tends to retain heat and often becomes combustible at high temperatures. Also, wires and connectors are frequently located in hot areas of the engine compartment or under the dash where there is little air circulation.

Because of these factors, very high resistance in any connector can produce high levels of heat and has the potential to cause a fire, especially if additional problems, such as a short circuit in the wiring or component, increase the load above normal levels. In addition, even if high levels of heat are avoided, high resistance in a wire or connector will inevitably deprive a light, motor or gauge of needed current and produce a vehicle operating problem.

In order to achieve successful diagnostic results, a technician should be familiar with the theory of electricity and understand basic electrical terms. Also, you should be familiar with testing equipment operation, and be able to measure voltage and resistance. You must know what happens in a circuit with a defective component or an open or shorted wire, and you must be able to read and understand a wiring diagram. Furthermore, diesel engine technicians should also be able to use jumper wires in order to make circuit checks.

In the event of a broken wire(s), a high quality splice is generally an acceptable fix to remedy this wiring harness problem. While some vendors maintain that shrink wrap is for the most part, the sealant of choice, electrical tape can be a suitable equivalent; rosin core solder and splice clips definitely enhance the seal's durability. Moreover, high quality splicing and wiring procedures are applicable to repair all wiring harnesses except the one connecting the ECM to the unit injectors. Splicing the ECM harness is not recommended; in the event of failure, it should be replaced.

When trying to diagnose an electrical problem, always approach the circuit in this manner:
- Determine the circuit power source
- Determine the circuit load(s)
- Determine ground.

OHM'S LAW

Ohm's Law can be used to help you figure circuit resistance, current flow or voltage if you know any two of these three values. This can help you in electrical troubleshooting. The basic formula is $E = I \times R$: E refers to voltage, I to current and R to resistance.

This form of the law will give you voltage if you know current and resistance. For example, it tells us that if you have 12 volts applied to a circuit with a resistance of 1 ohm, current flow will be 12 amps. That is 12 (volts) = 12 (amps) x 1 (ohm). A circuit with 2 ohms resistance would have a flow of 6 amps at 12 volts, because 12 (volts) = 6 (amps) x 2 ohms.

To find current flow when you know voltage and resistance use the formula this way: $I = E/R$. To find the resistance of the circuit when volts and amps are known, use $R = E/I$.

General Electrical System Diagnosis

MEASURING POWER

It can be useful to measure power for the purposes of establishing proper alternator and battery capacities. This becomes critical because of the number of options available for heavy trucks and the tendency for many truck users to add electrical equipment after the truck is built. If an alternator does not have sufficient capacity to replace all the energy used by the accessories, battery problems will result.

In cases where it becomes necessary to measure total power consumed by an accessory, it can be handy to understand the formula for power, P = I x E. P refers to power in watts, I refers to the current in amps, and E refers to the voltage in volts.

Consider a situation where a trucking company has added an auxiliary blower to help heat or cool the cab. Suppose the label on the motor gives its rating as 84 watts. However, most alternators are rated in amps. There is another version of the formula that can be used to calculate amps when the voltage and wattage are known. It is I = P/E. All the technician needs to do is divide power in watts (84) by the 14 volts in the system when the alternator is charging. We then simply divide 84 by 14 (P/E). This gives us the figure 6, which means that the motor draws 6 amps.

This figure could then be added to the other figures representing power drawn by the various accessories to determine the total power drawn. This total in amps could then be compared to the output of the alternator.

TESTING INSTRUMENTS

The meters commonly used by technicians to find chassis wiring or other electrical problems are the voltmeter, the ammeter and the ohmmeter. Functions for these meters are commonly combined into one unit called a digital multimeter, or DMM.

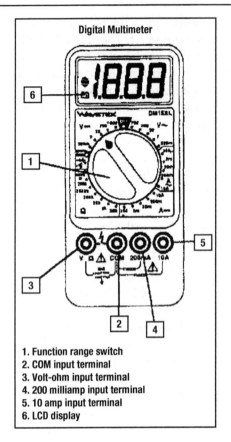

Digital Multimeter

1. Function range switch
2. COM input terminal
3. Volt-ohm input terminal
4. 200 milliamp input terminal
5. 10 amp input terminal
6. LCD display

DMMs read out via a display of numbers in digital form, and are the preferred meter to use with today's solid-state electronic systems. They are superior for testing electronic circuits because of their higher accuracy. A DMM will read the voltage no matter which way it is connected. If connected backwards, a (–) sign will precede the voltage readout, but the meter will not be damaged.

Some circuits are designed to carry very small amounts of current. For this reason, a high-impedance (over 10 megohms) digital meter must always be used when troubleshooting computer-related circuits.

Graphing Multimeters (GMMs) recognize the difference between normal and unusual signal patterns, with the capability of saving and storing data for analysis and repair. They translate an electronic signal into a waveform and display it on screen. As the waveform is displayed, it creates a signature of the signal's characteristics — including any intermittent problems that may be occurring. Most GMMs have a database that holds vehicle-specific information. Accessing the database allows the technician to review wiring diagrams, pin numbers and test procedures.

Although they should be limited in their usage, 12-volt test lights can come in handy when checking for voltage in non-digital circuits. A self-powered test light can also be used in non-digital circuits to help to diagnose a circuit that lacks voltage.

On some systems, a breakout box can be used to trace a fault in the wiring circuit. The breakout box is designed to probe electronic circuits from a position not integral with the engine compartment. It is connected to the vehicle and engine harnesses at the ECM.

Then, DMM probes can be connected to the specific

Graphing Multimeters (GMMs) display an electronic signal in waveform.
(Courtesy: OTC Tools Corp.)

General Electrical System Diagnosis

box sockets to isolate circuits in accordance with the manufacturer's wiring diagram and specifications.

VOLTAGE

Voltage is the electrical pressure behind the electron stream. Or, the potential, potential difference, or voltage drop that designates electric pressure between two or more points. It is the force that pushes electrons through conductors and loads. The units measured are called volts.

To check for certain non-digital voltage, (such as lighting) you can use a test light, consisting of a 12-volt light bulb with a pair of leads attached. To use the test light, ground one lead, and touch the other lead to various points along the circuit where voltage should be present. When the bulb lights, there is power at the point being tested. When you get to a point where there's no voltage, you know there's a problem between that point and the last point tested.

As often as possible, a DMM should be substituted for a 12-volt test light. While a test light indicates whether voltage is present, a DMM will tell you how much voltage is present.

If you are testing a circuit containing solid-state electronic components, you must use a DMM having an internal resistance of at least 10 megohms. Otherwise, damage to the solid-state component can result because of current flow it was not designed to carry.

Set the range switch to a range that covers a voltage higher than the voltage to be measured. For example, to measure battery output of about 12.6 volts, set the meter to a range covering 0-25 volts, rather than a lower range. A DMM won't be damaged if you set it to a range that is lower than required, but it will indicate over-range, and will not be able to measure the voltage in the circuit.

To measure voltage using a DMM, use the following steps:
1. Connect the red test lead to the V connector and connect the black lead to the COM input on the meter. If there is a DC AC switch, make sure it is switched to the DC position.
2. Set the function/range switch to the desired volts position. If the magnitude of the voltage is not known, set the switch to a range that will read the most voltage seen on the vehicle. (Normally, a 20V range will be sufficient). Reduce the range until you have a satisfactory reading.
3. Connect the red test or positive lead to a part of the circuit that carries voltage, and the ground or black lead to a known good ground, and read the digital display to obtain the voltage in the circuit.

Keep in mind that when using a GMM, you will be reading waveforms instead of numbers. These waveforms are the same as those found on an oscilloscope. The graphing multimeter will display voltage on the vertical scale and time along the horizontal scale.

VOLTAGE DROP

Additional resistance that should not be in a circuit can cause voltage drop. This means there will be less available voltage flowing in the circuit to perform its function. Voltage drops are usually caused by poor connections, such as corrosion in connectors, faulty solder joints, paint between a wiring connector and firewall, and so on.

A DMM is helpful in checking for voltage being lost along a wire or through a connection or switch. To do this, connect the positive lead of the meter to the end of the wire or to the side of the connector or switch that is closer to the battery.

Connect the negative lead to the other end of the wire (or the other side of the connector or switch). Now, operate the circuit while watching the meter. Because it is exposed to voltage through both its connectors, it will show the difference in voltage between the two points. For example, let's consider a length of wire receiving 12 volts at the end nearer the battery and carrying 10 volts to the connection at the switch. If connected to either end of this wire, the meter would read 2 volts. A difference or drop of more than one volt in one section of wire, or through one connector or switch, usually indicates a problem.

An alternate method for checking voltage drop is to ground the negative lead and take voltage measurements at several points along the circuit. The readings may vary by about one volt, especially when long wire runs (like trailer harnesses) are being tested. But if the difference is much greater, the circuit should be checked for bad connections or damaged wires.

AMPERES

The unit of measure for current flow is called amperes (or amps). The DMM should always be set to the highest amperage range before starting to take a measurement. Then, lower the setting until a usable reading is obtained. If the reading is more than half range on the DMM, don't switch to a lower range. A digital unit will not be able to give a reading if the amperage measured is out of range.

Connect the ammeter as you would a voltmeter, with the red or positive probe connected on the battery positive side of the circuit, and the negative lead toward the ground side of the circuit or the battery negative terminal. When working on the voltage side of the load, the negative lead would then be on the load side of the ammeter. If working on the ground side, the positive lead would be on the load side of the ammeter,

General Electrical System Diagnosis

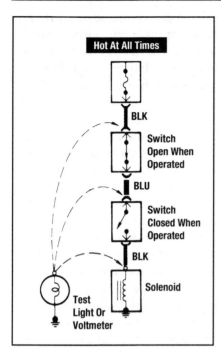

Testing for voltage with a test light.
(Courtesy: GM Corp.)

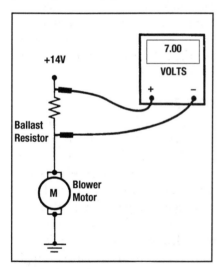

Connecting an analog voltmeter across a ballast resistor. Even though the ground or negative lead of the meter will be contacting a wire with voltage in it, the meter will not be damaged because the voltage on the battery side of the resistor, where the positive lead is connected, will be higher.
(Courtesy: Interstate Battery System of America)

and the negative lead would then be on the side away from the load.

Note that an ammeter is useless unless it is connected in series with the circuit so all the current passes through the ammeter. This means that the ammeter will complete the circuit.

RESISTANCE

The unit of measure for resistance to current flow is called ohms. An ohms setting on a DMM is different from the other two settings because it is directly connected to its own battery and supplies its own power. The battery energizes the circuit and the unit then measures flow.

You can use a DMM measure the resistance of a given component, or the resistance of an entire section of a circuit, from a point on the voltage side of the load, through the ground wiring and connections. In the first case, the leads are connected on either side of the component. In the second case, the positive lead is connected on the voltage side of the load and the negative lead to a good chassis ground.

To measure resistance, turn the power off in the circuit before connecting the meter. This will protect the circuits, which are designed to operate only at very low voltages. Then zero the ohmmeter. Connect the leads together and verify that the unit reads about 0.3 ohms, indicating the minimal resistance in the test leads.

When checking the resistance of a load, make sure there is no other resistor or component connected in parallel with the item being tested. Such a unit would have to be disconnected in order for you to get an accurate reading. Note the difference between an open and a short. An open circuit means infinite resistance.

NOTE: When measuring high resistance, be careful not to contact adjacent points, even if they are insulated. Some insulators have a relatively low insulation resistance, which can affect the measurement.

CONTINUITY

A DMM will register if a continuous electrical path exists. (If a path exists, the circuit is considered to have continuity). This continuity check can be used where the test is looking for greater than, less than or equal to 5 ohms. An open circuit (broken electrical path) would have resistance and would not have continuity.

To use the continuity feature of certain meters, perform the following procedure:

- Place the function/range switch in any range
- Connect the red lead to the V connector and connect the black lead to the com connector on the meter. With the test leads separated or measuring an out-of-range resistance, the digital display will indicate OL (over limit)
- Place one test probe at one end of the wire or circuit to be tested. Use the other test lead to trace the circuit. When continuity is established, a symbol will be displayed in the upper left corner of the digital readout. If contact in the wire is maintained long enough (about 1/4 of a second), the OL will disappear and the resistance value of the wire or circuit will be displayed next to the symbol.

If your DMM does not work as described above, you must learn how your DMM operates in order to use this procedure.

A self-powered test light can also be used on non-digital circuits. One lead of the self-powered test light should be touched to each point. If there is continuity, the test light's own circuit will be completed, and the bulb will light. Under these conditions, the test light replaces the battery and load of the circuit, and the portion of the vehicle circuit being tested becomes a part of the ground circuit.

General Electrical System Diagnosis

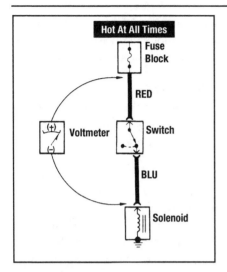

Voltage drop test.
(Courtesy: GM Corp.)

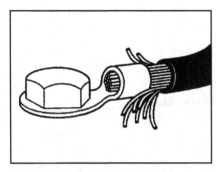

A defective ground connection can produce a voltage drop at the connector. Although some wires are still connected, several strands are broken loose.
(Courtesy: Interstate Battery System of America)

SHORTS

A short circuit, or short, is a connection of comparatively low resistance accidentally or intentionally made between points in a circuit where the resistance is normally high. Short circuits can occur in two different ways. There are shorts to ground, where the current bypasses to ground before it reaches the load that it was heading for, and there are shorts to power—that is, another power source in another circuit.

If a short to ground occurs before the load, the fuse should blow or the circuit breaker should trip. Shorts to another power source can cause operation of circuits when they are not necessarily supposed to be operating.

A short circuit to ground is most often caused by a failure in the wiring and its insulation. A DMM can be utilized to locate short circuits, in addition to other devices—appropriately called short finders—made for this purpose.

NOTE: *Blown fuses or breakers most often indicate a short circuit in the wiring. However, a short can occur inside a motor or light.*

OPENS

An open circuit, or open, is a situation where the continuous flow of electricity is interrupted.

To locate opens with a DMM, the first and most important detail is that all circuit power must be off. If the power is on, the technician could send too much voltage through the meter and damage it.

If a circuit contains an open at a certain point, a continuous circuit from the power source right to this point, when checked with a DMM, would register available voltage. On the other side of the open, voltage would not be present.

KEY-OFF BATTERY DRAIN (PARASITIC DRAW)

Parasitic draws are present when the vehicle is not running and an electrical circuit is operating when it is not supposed to operate. This contributes to battery depletion, even if the battery(s) are in good condition and the charging system is in proper working order.

In most cases, there will be a very slight draw on the battery because of computerized systems in the vehicle that need voltage at all times in order to function properly. Components such as computer memories and stored diagnostic data must be kept whether the vehicle is running or not. The alternator, voltage regulator, digital clock and other such items also draw a very small current

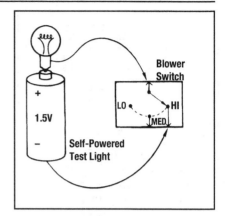

Testing for continuity with a self-powered test light.
(Courtesy: GM Corp.)

while the vehicle is off. This is not a problem for today's vehicles as long as the drain is not excessive.

Sometimes, it's hard to tell whether there is a key-off battery drain because the drain won't be enough to completely discharge the battery while the vehicle is off. The only way this type of drain manifests itself is by excessive battery water usage and the fact that the battery(s) don't last as long as they should with a known good charging and starting system.

Always use manufacturer's suggested key-off drain specifications when trying to determine the proper amount of current accessories should

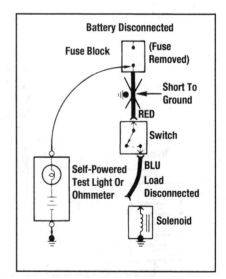

Locating a short to ground with a self-powered test light.
(Courtesy: GM Corp)

Training for Certification

General Electrical System Diagnosis

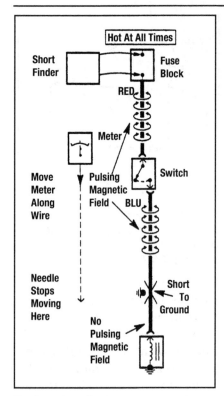

For locating shorts, connect a short finder directly into the fuse holder circuit. The short finder generates a pulsing magnetic field through the circuit, which can be traced with a meter. The pulse will endure as long as the circuit is grounded. From the point of the short, the pulse will cease.

draw when the vehicle's engine is not running. In addition, when adding non-OEM accessories to a vehicle, OEM key-off drain must be added to accessory key-off drain to see if the total is within specifications.

The most effective way of checking for a parasitic draw is to use a DMM, set to the amps mode, in series with the negative battery cable and the negative battery post. This enables full battery voltage to the vehicle during the measurement.

CAUTION: *Be careful when connecting an ammeter in series with the battery cable. Voltage spikes can blow the fuse and possibly damage the DMM.*

That said, special test adapters have been developed to alleviate the risk of damaging a DMM. These testers consist of a resistor pack, and are placed in series with the battery cable, and the DMM is connected to the test adapter to measure the voltage drop to determine the key-off drain measurement. Use the manufacturer's recommended specifications when using this type of test adapter.

If the key-off drain is in excess of 6.5 amps, the resistor pack of the test adapter can become damaged due to overheating. Therefore, it is not recommended to allow this high of a continuous drain to flow through the adapter for more than 1 minute.

NOTE: *Make sure the ignition switch is in the OFF position at all times during testing. In addition, all courtesy and accessory lights must be OFF.*

If an excessive drain is displayed, remove the fuses from the fuse block one at a time. When the specific fuse powering the circuit with the drain is removed, the high voltage reading will stabilize to a normal reading.

Using a wiring diagram, note the specific circuits that run to the particular fuse that was pulled. Reinstall the fuse and allow the DMM to read the excessive draw. Now, disconnect each circuit to further isolate the current draw. When the draw returns to normal, you've found the circuit that's causing the problem.

If the drain is not found using this procedure, use a wiring diagram and locate all circuits connected to the battery that use a fusible link. Disconnect the circuits, one at a time, to isolate the circuit with the excessive draw. A fusible link is a fused wire that protects a particular circuit from high currents, and may be either in a harness, or mounted separately, and performs the same function as the fuses in a fuse block.

DIODES

The battery and other electrical accessories operate on Direct Current (DC). Meaning, electricity flows in one direction only. For this reason it is necessary to change Alternating Current (AC) from the charging system to DC. This function is performed by rectifying diodes. The diode is an electrical device, which rectifies or changes alternating current to direct current by allowing current to freely pass through in one direction, but not the other. It acts much like an electronic check valve.

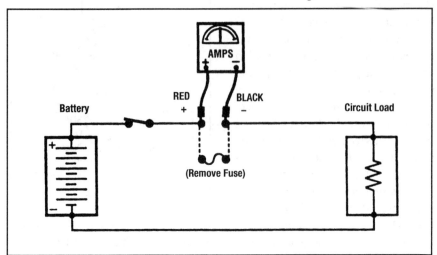

Connecting an ohmmeter across a section of circuit which has been opened for test purposes. *(Courtesy: Interstate Battery System of America)*

Since diodes are polarized, you will need to know which diodes go where before they are replaced. Negative diodes have black markings on the case and positive diodes have red markings. Except for this, the diodes look alike. Some diodes may be covered with red insulating paint, but the red and black diode markings should still show through. You should also note that the heat sink connected to the alternator output terminal is insulated from the alternator shell. The other heat sink is grounded to the shell. Since the ground polarity of this alternator is negative, the diodes mounted in the grounded heat sink must be negative (black). The diodes in the insulated heat sink must be positive (red).

Most DMMs have a diode testing function to avoid disconnecting the diode from the circuit wiring. If the diode fails open, the DMM will display an open circuit. If the diode fails closed, the DMM will display zeros. Commercially available testers can also be purchased to check diodes. Consult the tester instructions when using these testers.

CAPACITORS

A capacitor is a device that is used for holding or storing a surge of electrical current and releasing it as needed. It limits transient voltage across a circuit, thereby protecting components from damaging electrical surges. Applications that use capacitors include powertrain control, Antilock Brake Systems (ABS), traction control systems, supplemental restraint systems, driver information and diagnostics systems. Any of these applications may employ capacitors of all types and styles.

Capacitor resistance can be checked with a DMM. Connect one lead to the body of the capacitor and the other lead to the capacitor connector and read the resistance. Compare with manufacturer's specifications.

RESISTORS

Simply put, a resistor is an electrical component that causes resistance in a circuit. The specific resistance is caused by the collision of electrons. Resistors are installed in a circuit to limit current, drop voltage, divide voltage from a source into different portions, and discharge energy.

Resistors are normally described in terms of their electrical resistance in ohms and their ability to dissipate heat in to watts (power). They are also defined by their construction (composition, wire-wound, or film) and by their function (fixed or variable), and are rated with an inherent error factor.

Variable resistors are either composition type or wire-wound. They have a sliding contact so the amount of resistance can be changed. Low-powered resistors are called potentiometers. High-powered resistors are called rheostats.

Another resistor, called a thermistor, changes in accordance with temperature. Thermistors are composed of dual-wire electrodes bonded to semiconductor material. Thermistors are rated by their negative or positive coefficient of resistance. A negative coefficient means the thermistor lowers its resistance as temperature rises, and a positive coefficient means the thermistor raises its resistance as temperature rises.

Resistance values should be checked using a DMM set to the ohms position. Consult manufacturer's specifications for thermistor temperature ranges and ohms values before testing resistors.

RELAYS

Relays re designed so that a high amperage circuit can be turned on and off by a low current switch. When current flows through the coil of the relay, its core is magnetized, closing the contacts. When the current is removed, the contacts are returned to their original position using a spring.

Relays may be classified as NO (Normally Open) or NC (Normally Closed). Always consult the manufacturer's wiring diagram to ensure you understand the operation of the relay being tested.

Relays can be tested using a 12-volt source and a DMM. Connect the 12-volt source to the relay and check for continuity at the appropriate relay contacts as prescribed by the manufacturer. Refer to manufacturers specifications for specific values.

SOLENOIDS

A solenoid is an electromagnetic switch that converts an electrical signal into mechanical operation. Solenoids can be used in many ways, some of which include starter systems, injector controls, door lock actuators, etc.

To test a solenoid, make sure it is grounded and connect a positive jumper wire to the appropriate terminal of the solenoid. Connect the other end of the positive jumper wire to the appropriate voltage source, and check operation of the solenoid per manufacturer recommendations.

WIRING DIAGRAMS

When diagnosing electrical circuits, one important skill will be the ability to understand wiring diagrams. Since wiring diagrams are like a road map of the electrical system, trying to trace electrical problems without them makes the job twice as hard. Circuits in vehicles contain numerous components, and many different circuits may share some of the same wires.

Wiring diagrams indicate circuit identification factors like wire colors, connector types and locations. This is vital information when diagnosing electrical problems. But, before a technician begins his or her search, they must be certain that the diagram is in fact the correct one for the vehicle. Revisions and

General Electrical System Diagnosis

changes to wiring harnesses can take place, causing confusion. Also, always look for a legend on the wiring diagram indicating which symbols represent which components. Different manufacturers might use different symbols to represent the same components.

Review the table of symbols shown in this manual, and make it a point to learn the various ways different manufacturers typically show their circuits in manuals. Symbols are usually self-explanatory, such as the symbol for a bulb clearly showing the curl of the filament and the one for a battery looking like plates sandwiched together.

In every diagram, a line shown between symbols is an electrical pathway between components, usually a wire or cable. Sometimes, an entire group of circuits are summarized in a block or square on the diagram because too many components are contained within. Commonly, power connections are on the top and bottom of a schematic, and input and output circuits are depicted to the left and right, but all of this can vary with the particular schematic.

If simplified schematics aren't available for a given vehicle, don't be intimidated by the more complex type that shows several circuits lumped together. Make a photocopy of the schematic and highlight the circuit you are interested in. It's often helpful to redraw it on a separate piece of paper in simplified fashion. Straighten out the wires and arrange the components so you can understand the intended current path. This may seem like a lot of trouble, but a clear schematic can substantially shorten the diagnostic time.

Consider the following hypothetical service situation: A driver complains that a vehicle's high-beam lights don't work. The technician first makes his own observations about the problem. He operates the headlights and notes that the low beams do work. He operates the dimmer switch and notes that the high-beam indicator comes on, but the high beams themselves do not.

Since both high-beams are out, he suspects the problem is in an area common to both left and right high-beams—either power or ground (although it's possible, it's extremely unlikely that the high-beam portion of both headlights blew at the same time).

At this point, he consults the headlight schematic (see headlight schematic in this manual). With the light switch in the head position, and the dimmer switch in low, current should flow through the circuit breaker, light switch, yellow wire and the low contacts of the dimmer switch. It should then flow through the tan wires and connector C120, and through the low filament of each headlight to ground (G101 and G104).

Since this part of the circuit is working, the technician knows:
- Current is getting through the low part of the dimmer switch to the headlights
- The problem isn't a bad ground; otherwise, the low beams would not work either.

Back to the schematic. When the dimmer switch is in the high position, current should flow through

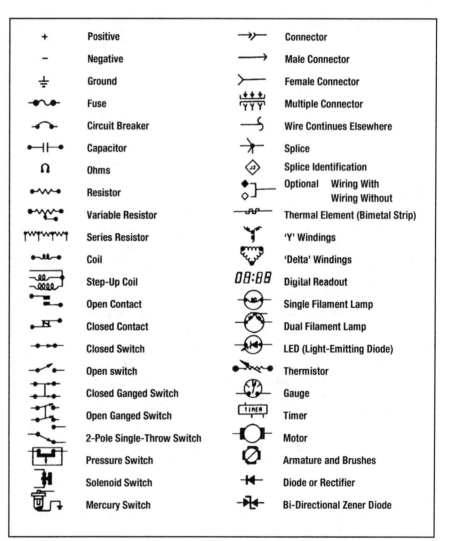

Typical electrical symbols used in wiring diagrams and schematics.

General Electrical System Diagnosis

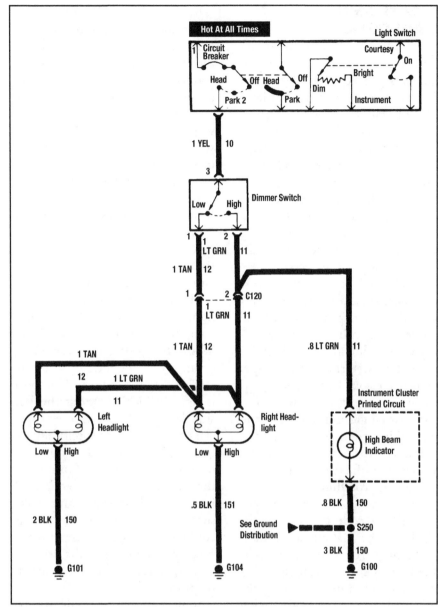

Typical headlight schematic. *(Courtesy: GM Corp.)*

the high contacts of the dimmer switch, and through the light green wire to connector C120. From there, the current path splits. Current should flow through one light green wire and the high-beam indicator to ground G100. It also should flow through connector C120 and the other light green wires, through the high filaments of the headlights, to grounds G101 and G104.

The technician is zeroing in. Remember, he observed that the high-beam indicator came on, although the high beams didn't. So he knows

there is power available at the upper half of connector C120. He also knows the grounds are good, since the low-beams share those grounds, and they work.

The technician concludes that the problem is either at the lower half of connector C120, or along the light green wire between connector C120 and the right-hand headlight. Note that the technician narrowed the problem to a specific area, without having done any work on the vehicle!

The next step would be to learn where connector C120 is located on

the vehicle. Most schematics have corresponding component location tables either appended or in accompanying service literature.

Using a 12-volt test light or multimeter to test the wire and connector, the technician can then pinpoint the problem and correct it. The final step should always be to thoroughly test the repair. Do the high beams and high-beam indicator work? Do the low beams still work? If so, the repair is complete.

MULTIPLEXING

The addition of multiplexing allows control components such as sensors and modules to communicate by transmitting digital data on one wire. This technology potentially eliminates the need of multiple wires, and reduces the cost, weight, and failures associated with these wires.

Multiplexing essentially involves sending multiple pieces of information on one wire (data bus). The separate signals are then recovered at the end of the signal transmission, or at the module.

The network widely in use today is called a Controlled Area Network (CAN). This is a high-speed engineering standard that is designed to allow computers to transmit information via the vehicle's data bus.

There are three different data buses, all with different speeds. A data bus with a class A speed rating is the slowest. This type of data bus is used for operating components such as power door locks and windows. A class B data bus has a higher speed rating and may be used for electronic instrumentation and climate control operation. The last speed rating, class C, is up to 100 times faster than the class B data bus. This system operates components that must activate immediately such as air bags, stability control and antilock brake systems.

General Electrical System Diagnosis

The most recent data bus system used by heavy-truck manufacturers is designated J-1939.

Each module is called a node, and is attached to the data bus. Each node sends and receives signals allowing it to function. Nodes possess a unique address, allowing all other irrelevant information to be ignored.

Keep in mind that while CAN-equipped vehicles carry less wiring, they also have more modules to malfunction, meaning proper diagnosis is critical. Connectors become more important than ever on CAN-equipped vehicles.

If a problem occurs, the first step is to find out whether the problem is static (always occurs) or dynamic (intermittent). If the problem is dynamic, chances are it's probably not a gauge or other electronic or mechanical component failure, but rather a wiring problem affected by vibration.

If the problem is dynamic, check all the ground connections to make sure the cab and chassis are properly grounded. Then, check all the connectors at the data bus to all the gauges, making sure all of them are tight. If these wiring checks fail to uncover the problem, use manufacturer's flow charts, wiring diagrams and diagnostic trees to narrow down the possibilities.

Fault diagnosis is essentially the same as with any non-CAN equipped vehicles. However, most current generation scan tools are incapable of diagnosing CAN systems. Therefore, when you purchase a scan tool, make sure it is CAN-compliant and comes with upgraded software. This will allow the tool to recognize CAN messages.

Just like with other electronic failures, a diagnostic trouble code will be set and the Malfunction Indicator Light (MIL) will be illuminated.

ELECTRONIC DIAGNOSTICS

As with any electronically controlled component, the best diagnostic procedure is to retrieve the particular fault code associated with the failure. Should a component act erratically, the ECM will record this fact and store or log a fault code that tells the technician what has occurred. The system's goal is to direct the technician to the problem, and retain information about an intermittent fault that may not be evident when the truck is brought in for service.

Check for loose or broken wire connections, and improperly formed or damaged terminals. All connector terminals in the problem circuit should be carefully inspected to determine the proper contact tension. Use a mating terminal to test contact tension. Ensure that all grounds are clean and are making good contact. If basic checks fail to locate the problem, follow manufacturer's electronic test system procedures.

When a fault is detected in a circuit, a fault code is stored in the ECU and the Malfunction Indicator Light (MIL) illuminates. Thus, one basic step in troubleshooting electronic circuits is reading the fault codes and interpreting what they mean.

The ECU stores two types of fault codes, inactive and active. Inactive codes describe malfunctions that may be intermittent. An intermittent code may be one that is set only when the vehicle is operated under certain conditions, such as when the vehicle is in motion, making turns, or travelling at a certain speed. Active codes are existing codes pertaining to a malfunction that happens all the time, no matter the conditions or driving speed. In either event, ECU trouble codes must be erased after the vehicle is repaired.

Remember, fault codes only point to the particular problem circuit. They don't necessarily tell you the exact component failure. Loose connections, broken wires, or improper peripheral component operation could cause malfunctions, so give the circuit a thorough visual inspection when diagnosing a malfunction.

If the truck has a diagnostic switch, shut down the engine and turn the ignition switch to the ON position. Turn on the diagnostic switch and hold it in the ON position until the MIL has finished flashing the stored codes.

The system can be tested by any number of commercially available computer programs or scan tools. With the ignition switch OFF, connect the computer or scan tool to the diagnostic port. This port is usually located under the left side dash panel, and requires a special connector made specifically for this purpose. Turn the computer or scan tool power on. Ensure that the diagnostic switch (if equipped) is in the off position, and make sure the computer or scan tool is configured in accordance with the specific circuit. As faults are displayed, continue with the diagnostic process.

Some software programs may be equipped with service procedures, enabling the technician to diagnose and repair the system with an electronic repair manual.

ECM trouble codes that are stored in memory are removable by either selecting an option on the diagnostic reader, or on some older models, disrupting the power source to the ECM for a short period of time. Of course, there is a distinct disadvantage to the latter procedure. If the codes are removed by someone, all history of electronic malfunctions stored in the ECM are also removed.

Battery And Starting System Diagnosis And Repair

According to U.S. Department of Transportation Federal Highway Administration (FHWA) Motor Carrier Safety Regulations, the battery or batteries, unless located in the engine compartment, must be covered by a fixed part of the vehicle, or a removable cover. In addition, any metal parts that might corrode due to battery leakage must be coated with acid-resistant paint.

The lead-acid storage battery is an electro-chemical device, which converts and stores electrical energy in the form of chemical energy, and reconverts it into electrical energy when a circuit across the terminal posts is closed.

The battery creates a difference of electrical potential between the terminal posts, through the chemical action of the electrolyte upon the active materials of the positive and negative plates, which are made of lead. The electrolyte solution is a combination of sulfuric acid and water. The lead/sulfuric acid chemistry of the battery dictates the voltage of one cell, which is approximately 2.11 volts at full charge. Thus, 12-volt batteries always contain six cells connected in series so the voltage builds up to the required value, giving 12.66 volts at full charge.

When the battery is charged, there are too many electrons on the negative plates and an insufficient number on the positive plates. So, an electrical pressure that attempts to force the electrons to flow from the negative to the positive plates exists. Since the electrolyte is an insulator, the only way the electrons can travel is through the wiring and accessories linking the positive and negative terminals.

Cold Cranking Amp (CCA) ratings help technicians choose the right battery for cold starting. CCA is the number of amps a battery can deliver for 30 seconds at 0°F, at 1.2 volts-per-cell or a terminal voltage of 7.2.

Reserve Capacity (RC) is another rating that expresses the battery's ability to provide small amounts of power for a long time without discharging to the point where sulfation damage will occur. This rating is valuable in choosing the right battery for applications where the driver may draw a small amount of power from the batteries overnight with the engine shut down. It was intended originally to rate the battery's ability to keep the vehicle operating after a charging system failure. Technically, this is the number of minutes the battery can deliver 25 amps at 80°F at 1.75 volts per cell or a terminal post voltage of 10.5 volts.

DEEP CYCLING

Proper battery maintenance consists primarily of protecting the battery from deep cycling, sulfation, overcharging and vibration. Deep cycling occurs when the battery is drained of all useful current and then recharged to its full value. The heat, stresses, expansions and contractions created in the process cause plate warpage and loss of active material. The extent of the damage depends upon the severity of the discharging, the rates of recharging, and how often the deep cycling occurs. It also depends on the type of battery being used. Special high cycle units will withstand regular discharging down to 60 percent of capacity. If batteries are failing due to deep cycling, they should be replaced with the correct type of unit.

Hard engine starting can drain a battery by requiring too much total voltage to be drawn out of it before charging begins to reverse the process. If the operator tries repeatedly to start the truck over a period of several hours, allowing the battery to recover between attempts, failure of the engine to start can thoroughly discharge the battery. A short or ground in the wiring or a defective unit in the electrical system can cause discharge when the truck sits overnight or longer with the engine shut down. The burning of lights or using other accessories for extended periods of time without the engine running are

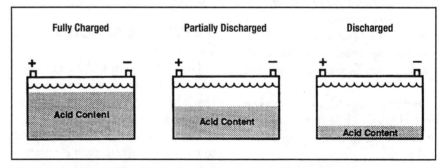

The acid content of the electrolyte drops during discharge, making the electrolyte mostly water. For this reason, deep cycling can cause batteries to freeze in frigid weather, causing damage to the plates or case.
(Courtesy: Interstate Battery System of America)

other major causes of deep cycling, since they may create an excessive drain on the battery over a long period of time, such as overnight.

Deep cycling has become more and more common as overnight idling has been reduced to save fuel and reduce emissions, while driver comfort items that draw power have seen increasing use. Deep cycling has the secondary consequence that it can cause the battery to freeze in cold weather. This happens because, as the battery is discharged, the amount of acid in the electrolyte drops. When the battery is discharged, the acid content is so low that the remaining electrolyte, now mostly water, can freeze.

BATTERY TESTING AND REPLACEMENT

At one time, many technicians believed that if batteries were placed on concrete, they would discharge faster than batteries kept on wood or other materials. In fact, because of the porous characteristics of the types of cases used in the past, tiny amounts of acid would drain through, removing the charge. These days, this condition is rare because of the polypropylene plastic cases being used for modern batteries.

WARNING: The sulfuric acid in battery electrolyte can cause serious injury if it contacts the eyes or skin. To prevent injury, always wear skin and eye protection when servicing batteries. Batteries also give off hydrogen gas, which can be explosive. Never smoke or allow open flames near a battery.

Batteries should always be kept fully charged while in storage. Batteries stored in a discharged state will sulfate.

BATTERY STATE OF CHARGE

The cranking output obtained from the starter motor is affected by the condition of the charge of the battery or by high resistance in the wiring. The voltage rating of the battery must also match the voltage rating of the starter motor.

To determine the battery state of charge using a DMM, make sure the battery is at rest for several hours. This allows the chemistry to settle down to its true level. Connect the DMM positive (red) lead to the positive terminal of the battery, and connect the negative lead (black) to the negative terminal of the battery. Compare the DMM voltage reading to the state of charge chart.

STATE OF CHARGE DETERMINED BY VOLTAGE

State of Charge	Voltage
100%	12.66
75%	12.45
50%	12.24
25%	12.06
Discharged	11.89

You should remember that when a battery's state of charge is checked with a DMM, the measurement obtained would not tell you whether or not you have a weak or defective cell. When replacing batteries, make sure the new unit(s) have adequate CCA and RC for the particular application. Always disconnect the negative cable first, and then the positive.

BATTERY CAPACITY TESTING

The battery should be checked and charged as needed before testing. The starter may not operate if the voltage at the battery is below 9.6 volts. Be sure the battery is rated to meet or exceed the vehicle manufacturer's recommendations.

Most high-rate discharge test equipment will measure the battery voltage while discharging the battery at a high rate through a fixed resistance for a few seconds. The resistance should be adjusted to limit the discharge to three times the battery ampere-hour rating. During this time, the voltage of a 12-volt battery should be 9.6 volts. Low voltage readings indicate the battery does not have sufficient discharge capacity for dependable performance. The battery may be undercharged, defective, or both.

BATTERY REPLACEMENT

Always mark the positive cable to prevent reverse-polarity connection upon installation. Also note that when a new battery is teamed up with several older units, it will tend to carry a load greater than that for which it was designed. It will be doing part of the work that should be done by the other units, and therefore may fail prematurely. It is recommended to replace all the batteries at the same time.

CAUTION: When removing the negative battery cable, make sure to maintain good contact between the cable clamp and the terminal post. This will prevent repeated voltage spikes that can damage engine or vehicle electronics.

After removing the cables and hold down, use a suitable battery carrier to remove the battery from the tray. This not only facilitates easier removal, but also helps to prevent electrolyte spillage. Once the battery is removed, inspect the battery box or tray, and clean all corrosion from the area (along with any hold-down brackets) with a baking soda solution. Inspect the cable connections again, checking that the ground connection is good at the frame, and the positive cable connection is secure. Clean the battery cables and clamps, especially at the terminal contact area.

Inspect the battery box or tray for any debris that may have collected

Battery & Starting System Diagnosis And Repair

while the vehicle was in use. Also, make sure the compartment is secure on its mountings and repair as necessary.

Install the battery, paying close attention to vehicle polarity. Although rare, some vehicles have positive grounded electrical systems. This is important because positive ground systems will require that the battery positive terminal be connected to a ground wire, and negative terminal to the cable that supplies the vehicle's accessories and connects to the alternator.

NOTE: Make sure that when batteries are installed, they do not come in contact with any other component on the vehicle other than the battery tray, cable connections and hold-downs.

After verifying the proper connections, connect the positive terminal first, then the negative, and tighten the connections. Next, install or replace battery hold-downs to ensure that there is no battery movement during vehicle operation.

CAUTION: Although often neglected, battery hold-downs play an important role in effective battery maintenance. Should a battery become loose due to a broken or missing battery hold-down, battery terminal contact with any metal component will cause serious electrical damage.

Vibration also tends to shake the active material out of battery plates, crack plate grids, separate plates from post straps, loosen terminals, and can even crack the battery case itself.

Be sure batteries are clamped in their trays tightly enough to hold them securely in place. Do not over-tighten. Over-tightening can distort and crack the battery cases.

BATTERY COMBINATIONS

When greater electrical power is needed, batteries are combined in series or parallel circuits to increase either the available voltage or the electrical reserve. When combining batteries in a series circuit, double the voltage is obtained. For example, two 12-volt batteries in series produce a large 24-volt battery.

Two 12-volt batteries wired in parallel will still yield 12 volts, but with greater reserve capacity. Multiple batteries are often connected in parallel in heavy-duty truck applications. When testing has indicated one or more defective batteries in a group, it is wise to replace all the batteries unless the others are new. Older batteries whose performance has begun to deteriorate will place an excessive load on new units, often resulting in premature failure.

BATTERY CHARGING

The battery should be maintained in a fully charged condition at all times to prevent sulfation and to ensure the availability of an adequate source of electric power. Because sulfation is a product of both low charge level and time, a discharged battery should be charged as soon as possible after the condition is noticed.

Jumping a discharged battery to start an engine, and then depending upon the vehicle charging system to charge the battery may prove satisfactory on an over-the-road vehicle during daylight hours in warm weather. Alternators used in heavy-duty applications work hard and are typically sized for the primary purpose of running the vehicle's accessories. If the alternator is used to charge the batteries after they have been drained, it will very likely be damaged through overheating, especially if accessory use is heavy.

For these reasons, charging a partially or fully discharged battery with a low-rate slow charger will produce the best results, minimizing the chances of a later no-start condition as well as the probability of creating further damage to the electrical system.

A battery is considered fully charged when its specific gravity remains uncharged during three consecutive readings taken at one-hour intervals even though a slow charger is connected. In general, charging is complete if a constant-voltage charger's output has dropped to 2-3 amps for a period of one hour.

It is best to wear safety goggles when working around charging batteries. Fill standard cells to the correct level with distilled water so gases can be vented. Securely replace caps as they are designed to isolate the gases from sparks.

NOTE: Make sure the charger is unplugged before connecting it to the battery terminals.

In general, it is best to use a constant-voltage charger. The constant-voltage unit reduces power as the battery approaches full charge. This helps to prevent overcharging. The total amount of time required to charge a battery varies with the degree of discharge. Assuming the battery is down to only 25 percent of its maximum charge, a slow charge would take 10 hours for an 80-minute reserve capacity unit; 15 hours for a 125-reserve capacity unit; and 20 hours for a 170-minute unit. Fast charging means one-fourth the time for each battery rating.

JUMP STARTING

Even the most experienced technician can incorrectly connect cables when jump starting a vehicle. When using another vehicle to jump-start a battery, make sure the distance between the jumper battery and the dead battery is as short as possible, without letting the vehicles contact each other. Turn off the source vehicle.

Battery & Starting System Diagnosis And Repair

Connect the positive (red) jumper cable to the positive terminals of both the dead and the source batteries, and then connect the negative (black) to the negative terminal of the source battery, and to a good ground on the vehicle with the dead battery. Make sure this connection is made away from the battery, as sparks could be emitted.

After verifying that the connections are properly made, start the source vehicle, and hold the rpm at around 2000 while the dead battery begins to charge. Cold temperatures and battery time of discharge will govern how long it will take to charge. Start the vehicle with the dead battery. As soon as the engine is running, disconnect the jumper cables from the source battery, and then from the battery that has been jumped.

LOW VOLTAGE DISCONNECT

Low voltage disconnect systems are designed to separate the load from the battery if battery voltage falls below manufacturer's specifications. This helps to prevent battery deep cycling.

The low voltage disconnect is installed inline between the battery(s) and the load. The disconnect is equipped with a sensor that monitors battery voltage, and cuts power to the load if battery voltage drops below a predetermined level. After battery voltage increases to yet another predetermined level, voltage is restored to the load.

Low Voltage Disconnect System malfunctions include voltage drops due to loose or corroded connections, misadjusted cutoff levels, or a defective voltage-sensing unit.

STARTING SYSTEM

When trouble develops in the starting system, such as the starter motor cranking the engine slowly or not at all, several preliminary checks can be made to determine whether

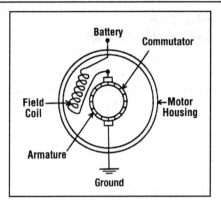

The wiring of a typical series-wound starter. The current flows from the battery through the field coils, then through the armature, and on to ground, to return to the battery. The commutator links the field coils with the armature.
(Courtesy: Interstate Battery System of America)

the trouble is in the battery, starting motor, wiring circuits, switches, or elsewhere.

Make certain the engine crankcase is filled with the proper weight motor oil as recommended by the engine or vehicle manufacturer. Heavier-than-specified motor oil, when coupled with low operating temperatures, will drastically lower cranking speed to the point that the engine will not start.

Other conditions aside from defects within the cranking motor can result in poor cranking performance. These may include engine problems or a dragging clutch. All tests should be made with the starter, engine and battery at room temperature (approximately 70°F).

Engage the starter and listen for any unusual scraping, grinding or rattling noises. Also, take notice of the torque on the starter. Note any starter drag and starting difficulty.

Use the following checks when troubleshooting for symptoms of starting system problems:

Engine will not crank
- One or more dead batteries
- Loose, broken or corroded connections and terminals
- Defective ignition switch
- Defective neutral switch
- Defective magnetic relay or solenoid
- Defective starter
- Internal engine damage.

Engine cranks slowly
- Insufficient battery state of charge
- Loose, broken or corroded connections and terminals
- Engine oil viscosity to thick
- Inappropriate cable size or routing
- Defective starter
- Internal engine damage.

Starter engages but engine won't crank
- Missing or damaged flywheel or flex plate teeth
- Worn or damaged starter gear.

Starter motor noise
- Worn or damaged starter gear
- Missing or damaged flywheel or flex plate teeth
- Loose starter
- Internal starter damage.

CRANKING VOLTAGE

This test will determine if sufficient battery voltage is available to operate the starting system.

On negative ground systems, connect the positive voltmeter lead at the starter's main (M) connector on the solenoid or motor body. This is the output of the solenoid, not the main battery cable connection. Then, connect the negative voltmeter lead at a good ground on the frame or body.

On positive ground systems, the voltmeter's positive terminal should be connected to a good ground on the frame or body, and the negative terminal should be connected to the starter's main (M) connector. A positive ground system can be identified by the fact that the battery terminal will be connected to a wire that is

24 T6 - Electrical/Electronic Systems

Battery & Starting System Diagnosis And Repair

grounded to the frame, rather than feeding to the alternator.

Disconnect the ignition system on gasoline engines and the fuel supply to diesel engines to prevent an accidental starting of the engine. Crank the engine and observe the voltmeter reading.

The voltmeter reading should be 9.6 volts or more, when testing a 12-volt system. If a reading of less than 9.6 volts is obtained, proceed with further testing.

VOLTAGE DROP

Excessive resistance in the starting system will cause slow cranking speeds and hard starting. Corrosion, loose terminals, loose, broken, damaged or undersized cables, or a loose starter motor on the engine block can cause this excessive resistance. In addition, the switches or relays involved must make good electrical connections when closed. The voltage drop test can be performed in three areas: the cranking circuit, the ground circuit and the control circuit.

Be aware that excessive voltage drop may mean the cables are simply undersized for the application. When replacing cables, all connections should be both crimped and soldered.

To check for voltage drop in the cranking system, perform the following procedure:

Set the DMM to read voltage and connect the black lead to the battery cable connection at the starter. Make sure the test point is positioned after the starter relay.

NOTE: The leads would have to be reversed should the vehicle have a positive ground system.

Disable the injection system to prevent the engine from starting. Have an assistant crank the starter motor. While the starter motor is cranking, touch the red lead of the DMM to the positive post of the battery. Adjust the DMM voltage scale to progressively lower scales until a reading can be viewed.

NOTE: When the DMM lead is connected to any point on the starter side of the solenoid or relay, battery voltage will be indicated on the voltmeter scale. This voltage will drop to the resistance value of the circuit when the starter is operated.

CAUTION: Do not turn the DMM to the low scale (2 volts) until the starter is in operation. Return the scale to the high side before the starter operation is completed to avoid damaging the voltmeter.

A reading of no more than 0.5 volts is permissible. If more than 0.5 volts is indicated, excessive resistance exists in the circuit.

Moving the black lead from the battery cable connection at the starter and checking each connection and cable back towards the battery can locate the excessive resistance point. When a noticeable decrease in the voltage reading is obtained, the trouble will be located between that point and the point previously checked.

Repeat the test so as to measure the voltage at the main terminal leading into the starter solenoid. If the voltage there is more the 0.2 volts above what was at the starter housing positive terminal, test the solenoid. Repair the connection as required and recheck. Values of maximum voltage drops for a typical standard 12V cranking system are as follows:

```
Cable under 3 ft. . . . . . . 0.1 volt
Cable over 3 ft. . . . . . . . 0.2 volts
Mechanical switches . . . 0.1 volt
Solenoid switches . . . . . 0.2 volts
Magnetic switches . . . . 0.3 volts
Each connection . . . . . . . . 0 volts
```

When testing the circuit, add the test results together. The total value should not exceed 0.5 volts. High resistance in the ground circuit of the starting system will result in hard starting and could also affect the charging system. To check for voltage drop in the ground circuit, perform the following procedure:

Set the DMM to read voltage and connect the red lead to a ground point on the starter and the black lead to the ground post of the battery.

Disable the injection system and have an assistant crank the engine. A voltage drop of 0.2 volts is permissible, but if higher than 0.2 volts, a poor ground circuit is evident and must be repaired. Causes could be

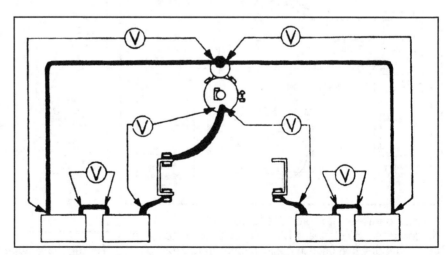

Make checks of voltage drop between all the points shown. These tests will find high resistance in any parts of the circuits feeding voltage to, and grounding the starter. *(Courtesy: Prestolite Electric, Inc.)*

Training for Certification 25

Battery & Starting System Diagnosis And Repair

a loose starter, or corroded or loose ground cables to the engine or frame. To provide a complete circuit, ground straps may be used at all these locations. However, if the vehicle has seen major work, critical ground straps may have been removed and not replaced. Look for signs that straps have been removed or disconnected, and make appropriate repairs.

The point or area of excessive voltage drop is located by moving the red DMM lead progressively closer to the battery one connection at a time and repeating the test, to check both connections and cables or straps. Be aware that if straps that formerly connected the engine to the frame or the starter to the engine have been removed, resistance may be obvious between those components, and new straps may have to be installed to correct the problem.

High resistance in the control circuit will reduce the current flow through the solenoid or relay windings, causing the solenoid or relay to not function properly, resulting in burned contacts within the units.

The end result is high resistance within the starting circuit. Poor supply of power to the solenoid may also create incorrect indexing of the starter pinion gear, making it impossible for the starter to engage the flywheel ring gear when it has stopped in some positions. To check for voltage drop in the control circuit, perform the following procedure:

- Locate the solenoid or relay, controlling switches and connections for the starting system. Observe the battery polarity. With negative ground systems, connect the DMM positive lead to the battery positive terminal, and the black or ground lead to the solenoid or relay switch terminal (the connector for the wire from the ignition switch).
- With positive ground systems, connect the black (ground) voltmeter lead to the battery negative post and the positive (red) lead to the solenoid or relay switch terminal.
- Disable the system so the engine will not start. Then, have an assistant crank the engine. Observe the voltmeter scale.
- If the voltmeter shows less than 0.5 volts, the circuit is in good condition; if it shows more than 0.5 volts; excessive resistance is present in the system.
- Isolate the point of high resistance by placing the DMM leads across each component in the circuit, in turn. A reading of more than 0.1 volt across any one wire or switch is usually an indication of a trouble area. The location of the voltage drop will determine which component must be replaced.

SERIES-PARALLEL SWITCHES

Series-parallel switches make it possible to electrically place batteries in series only during operation of the cranking motor, while retaining 12-volt power output during operation of the vehicle. This way, standard accessories can be used throughout the vehicle.

Series-parallel switches can be tested without removing them from the vehicle. However, you must be

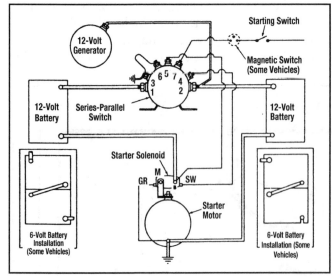

A series parallel switch provides 12 volts while de-energized, 50 standard 12-volt circuit components can be used, but when used in conjunction with two 12-volt batteries, can provide 24-volt power for starting very large displacement diesel engines.
(Courtesy: Interstate Battery System of America)

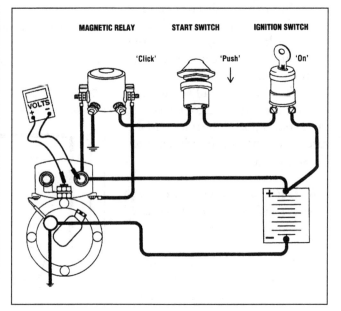

Testing the voltage drop across the solenoid contact disc to make sure full voltage is reaching the starter motor through the solenoid.
(Courtesy: Interstate Battery System of America)

Battery & Starting System Diagnosis And Repair

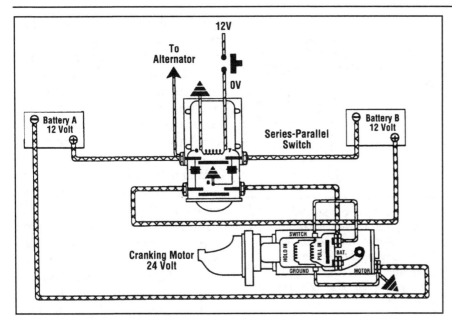

Series parallel switch when charging. The switch is de-energized, connecting the batteries in parallel for charging.
(Courtesy: Interstate Battery System of America)

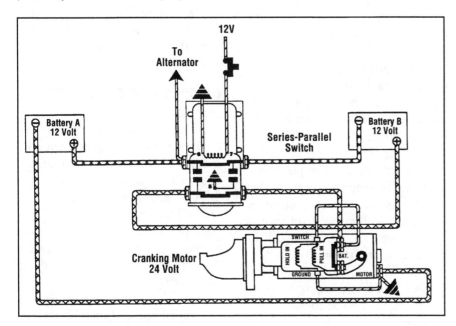

Series parallel switch when cranking. The switch is energized, connecting the batteries in series for 24-volt cranking.
(Courtesy: Interstate Battery System of America)

sure to test for a charging system problem with the switch in the starting or closed mode. To test a switch, it is necessary to perform a series of voltage drop measurements across the closed contacts of the switch.

To test the switch's performance during charging, run the engine and connect a DMM across the terminals of each battery. If the voltage is the same, the switch is functioning correctly in the charging mode. If it is lower on one battery than on the other, there is resistance through the part of the switch feeding the battery with the lower voltage.

To test further, connect the DMM between the positive battery terminal of each battery and the output terminal of the alternator. The reading (voltage drop) should not exceed 0.3 volts. To test the ground, connect the DMM between the alternator ground terminal and the negative terminal of each battery. Here, the difference should not be greater than 0.3 volts.

MAGNETIC RELAY

Many heavy-duty truck starting systems use a magnetic relay to switch the starter current on and off to provide voltage more consistently.

NOTE: Some magnetic relays are located in the engine compartment and some are integrated with the starter assembly. If the magnetic relay is integrated with the starter, the system is called an Integrated MAG system, or IMS.

Depending on the system, the relay may handle starter current directly or actuate the starter through the solenoid. Check for adequate voltage leading to the positive winding terminal on the relay, which is fed by the hot wire from the dash switch. With the DMM set on voltage and connected between this terminal and a good ground, have an assistant crank the engine. There should be 9-11 volts at this terminal.

Test the voltage between the negative winding terminal of the relay and a good ground, again with the voltmeter connected between this terminal and a good ground. Voltage must not exceed 0.1 volts, indicating an effective ground.

Also, check the voltage drop between the main terminal fed by the battery and the main output terminal feeding the starter or solenoid on the opposite side. With the starter operating, the voltage drop reading must not exceed 0.2-0.3 volts. If voltage is higher than this, the contact disc has developed high resistance due to burning.

Training for Certification — 27

Battery & Starting System Diagnosis And Repair

If the unit operates poorly or fails to close its contacts at all, you can also check the resistance of the windings with a DMM. With the unit de-energized (key switch OFF), connect the meter across the two winding terminals. Resistance should be approximately 0.80 ohms. Infinite or near zero resistance indicates an open or short, and a defective winding. Since resistance varies, read the resistance of a new relay of the type being checked to find out what normal resistance should be before condemning the unit.

To replace the relay, disconnect the negative battery cable. Next, mark and remove the wires from the relay. Loosen the fasteners and remove the relay from its mounting in the engine compartment.

NOTE: The starter must be removed to replace an integrated magnetic relay.

Before installing a replacement relay, check all cables and connections for corrosion and proper routing. Clean and make repairs as necessary. To install the relay, reverse the removal procedure. Reinstall the starter if removed.

STARTER SOLENOID

NOTE: Some manufacturers recommend replacing the starter and solenoid as a unit since they are most likely the same age and have been subject to the same conditions.

There are three basic voltage checks that should be made on the starter solenoid. Each should be made with the starter energized. First, test the voltage between the S terminal on the solenoid (coming from the relay or start switch) and a good ground. Voltage should be above 9.6 volts. If the voltage is below 9.6 volts, and the batteries

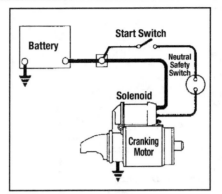

As starter-mounted solenoids energize, the starter switch provides starter motor current, and integral linkage provides starter drive engagement to the flywheel.
(Courtesy: Interstate Battery System of America)

are properly charged, the problem may be resistance in the wiring of the control circuit or a bad magnetic relay. If the voltage is high, the starter is not drawing power.

Test the voltage between the solenoid winding ground circuit G connector and ground. Voltage here should not be above 0.1 volt. If it's too high, correct a defective winding ground circuit.

Also, test the voltage drop between the solenoid B terminal (coming from the magnetic relay or start switch) and the terminal on top of the motor itself. The drop should be no more than 0.2 volts. If it is, and the solenoid winding is getting proper voltage and has a good ground, replace the solenoid or repair its internal disc contact.

NOTE: Most of the time, the starter must be removed to replace the solenoid. However, occasionally this procedure can be performed with the starter still mounted to the engine.

Disconnect the negative battery cable. Mark and remove the wires from the starter solenoid. If necessary, remove the starter from the vehicle. Remove the mounting bolts for the solenoid. It is possible that you may have to rotate the solenoid to remove it from the starter assembly, as some solenoids have a tab that fits in the starter housing. In addition, the plunger spring puts a slight tension on the solenoid and care must be taken upon removal so as not to lose the spring.

When installing the solenoid, make sure the spring is in place between the plunger and the solenoid body. Hold the solenoid and compress the spring. Note that you may have to rotate the solenoid to install it onto the housing just as you did when removing. If this is the case, make sure the tab of the solenoid fits down into the starter housing slot (if equipped). Install the attaching screws and if removed, install the starter assembly. Reconnect the starter wires and the negative battery cable and check for proper operation.

CRANK INHIBIT SYSTEM

Some trucks are equipped with a cranking inhibit system that keeps the starter from being accidentally cranked when the engine is running. This helps to reduce damage to the flywheel and starter drive gear.

The ECM reads various engine functions to determine if the engine is running. It then cuts voltage to the starter relay to prevent accidental cranking.

When the inhibit system experiences a malfunction, a trouble code is sent to the ECM. Connect a suitable scan tool to the diagnostic data link and read active or stored diagnostic codes. Compare these codes with the manufacturer's trouble code list.

THERMAL OVER CRANK PROTECTION

In order to prevent malfunctions related to starter overheating, some manufacturers have equipped starters with over crank protection (OCP). An over crank protected starter is equipped with an integrated circuit breaker that trips, cutting voltage to the relay when the starter is excessively overheated.

A starter can overheat when there is resistance or any other malfunction that would cause longer than normal engine cranking durations. Over crank protection ensures that the starter motor only operates under its normal working temperature. The circuit breaker will reset once the starter reaches a normal specified operating temperature.

CAUTION: Regardless of the starter construction, do not operate the starter for more than 30 seconds at a time without allowing it to cool for a minute or two. Overheating the starter by excessive cranking will severely damage the unit.

STARTER REPLACEMENT

Disconnect the negative battery cable. Label and disconnect the wires from the starter. Remove the bolts and shims or spacer washers (if equipped) and remove the starter assembly. Look for damaged or missing gear teeth on the flywheel or flex plate ring gear, and replace it if necessary.

When installing a replacement starter, be sure to use the same thickness of starter shims or spacer washers (if equipped) as the ones removed to prevent starter motor damage. After mounting the starter, torque the bolts to manufacturer's specifications. Reconnect the wires at the starter and the negative battery cable. Check for proper operation.

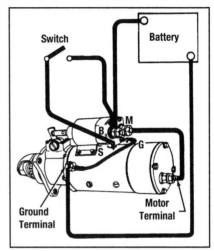

Heavy-duty starters are utilized on many high-compression diesels. The integral solenoid of this starter has an external ground circuit to the side of the starter motor.

Notes

Charging System Diagnosis And Repair

There are many different types of alternators available, ranging from a rated output of 35 to over 145 amps, depending upon the electrical demand of the vehicle. The voltage control regulators are mostly internal. However, there are still some externally mounted voltage regulators.

Mechanical energy is converted into electrical energy via the alternator. The alternator must produce enough electrical energy to maintain the vehicle battery in a correct state of charge, as well as supply the electrical energy required to operate all the other electrical equipment in the vehicle.

The principle by which the alternator converts mechanical energy into electrical energy is called electro-magnetic induction. This is a process in which a rotating magnetic field carried by field coils on the rotor cuts through stator windings connected to a load. When this happens, current is generated in the stator windings, and the torque required to turn the rotor that carries the field is increased.

Another type of alternator, called remote sensing, improves upon charging by recognizing actual load need instead of charging at a standard alternator output. This type of alternator bases its output on such variables as required voltage and ambient temperature.

Load sensing alternators are connected directly to the battery(s), allowing the voltage regulator to monitor the capacity of the battery(s) more closely. Once a voltage variance is detected, the field current is increased or decreased in proportion with the need.

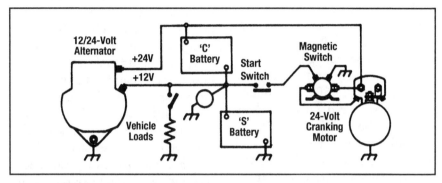

For vehicles with a 24-volt cranking motor, an alternator may produce two outputs, thanks to a transformer/rectifier unit. The integral unit converts and rectifies the alternator output for the dual requirements of 12 and 24 volts.

Alternator components are generally basic in their design and operation, but the physical appearance of each component will vary, depending on the application. The major components are as follows: the rotor, stator, diode rectifiers, heat sinks, brushes and alternator housing.

PRELIMINARY PROCEDURES

Before starting any charging system tests, consider the following list of important factors:
- Make sure there is sufficient battery state of charge
- Check and clean the terminal connections and posts
- • Clean and tighten wiring connectors at the alternator
- If the alternator is remote sensing, inspect the connections at the battery and alternator
- Make sure the alternator belts are in good condition and tightened properly
- Make sure the pulley(s) are aligned and properly mounted
- Make sure the alternator is mounted properly and brackets are secure
- Make sure all ground straps are in place and secure
- Disconnect the battery cables, check the physical, chemical, and electrical condition of the battery
- Be absolutely sure of polarity before connecting any battery in the circuit. Reversed polarity will ruin the diodes
- Never use a battery charger to start the engine
- Never ground the alternator output or battery terminal
- When making engine idle speed adjustments, always consider potential load factors that influence engine rpm. To observe the effects of an electrical load, switch on the lights, radio, heater, air conditioner, etc.

If the alternator is noisy, it may be caused by loose mounting bolts, a loose drive pulley, worn or dirty bearings, a defective diode or a grounded or shorted stator. If the noise continues after checking the mounting bolts and the pulley, the alternator must be replaced.

Charging System Diagnosis And Repair

CHARGING GAUGES AND WARNING LIGHTS

Voltage Gauge

The dash mounted voltage gauge measures charging system performance. When the batteries are fully charged, the dash gauge should read around 12.5 volts with the engine off. This is considered to be the base voltage. After the engine is started, and the rpm is raised to around 1500, the voltage gauge should read no more than 2.0 volts above the base voltage. It should remain at this rate unless significant loads such as lights, heater, or wipers are operating at the same time.

When this occurs, voltage should not drop below 12.5. This indicates proper operation of the charging system. If the gauge reads lower than 12.5 volts, this means that the battery(s) and not the alternator are providing current to the accessories. This is often the cause of dash and accessory light dimming on deceleration, and will eventually discharge the battery(s).

If the voltage gauge consistently reads below 14 volts, the charging system, wiring and/or gauge should be checked. If the voltage gauge reads above 15 volts, suspect a defective voltage regulator. If, after you've found the charging system working properly and the gauge is still reading low, suspect corroded or loose gauge wiring or a defective gauge. To test the gauge, perform a voltage drop test across the gauge circuit and compare readings to manufacturer's specifications.

Amp Gauge

The amp gauge reads current flow through the charging system. If the ammeter is reading negative amps, this means that the battery(s) and not the alternator are providing current to the accessories. This will eventually discharge the battery(s).

Normal readings should be at zero, slightly on the positive side of the gauge, if the battery(s) are fully charged and there is no electrical demand on the system. After the vehicle is started, the ammeter should read high positive amperage for a brief period of time. This is due to the increased current flow from recharging the battery(s) after start up. If the amp gauge consistently reads high as the vehicle continues to run, inspect the battery(s) for proper charge. If the amp gauge consistently reads negative and all charging system components have been checked out, suspect corroded or loose gauge wiring, or a defective gauge.

Warning Light

The warning light system depends on opposing voltages. If alternator output is less than battery voltage, the charging system warning light is activated by the difference in voltage sensed by the voltage regulator. If there is a problem in the charging system, the voltage regulator grounds the light circuit and illuminates the light.

A defective bulb can be detected by turning the ignition key to the START position without starting the engine. The warning light should illuminate. If it does not, suspect a defective bulb.

There are instances when the charging system warning light will illuminate when there is nothing wrong with the system. This can indicate a short in the warning light circuit, and not a charging system problem.

CHARGING SYSTEM DIAGNOSIS

Use the following checks when troubleshooting for symptoms of charging system problems:

Insufficient charging output (undercharge)
- Loose or worn alternator belt(s)
- Loose or corroded connections
- Defective alternator.

Higher than normal charging system output (overcharge)
- Defective voltage regulator
- Voltage drop in the alternator circuit.

Warning light on or voltage gauge reads low
- Missing alternator belt
- Damaged or disconnected wires
- Defective alternator or voltage regulator
- Defective gauge.

High-pitched squeal on acceleration or engine starting
- Loose alternator belt(s)
- Incorrect belt(s) for application (too large)
- Misaligned pulley(s).

Alternator noise
- Loose alternator mount or bracket
- Loose pulley(s)
- Worn internal components.

Connect a DMM set to volts to the battery posts and read the battery state of charge. Start the engine and operate it at approximately 1500 rpm under no electrical load except the ignition system. The voltage should increase, but not more than 2.0 volts above base.

NOTE: This is a good time to inspect the remote sense lead to the battery. While the engine is running, gently wiggle the connections at both the battery and alternator while viewing the voltmeter for fluctuating voltage.

The remote sense is also designed to monitor small voltage

Charging System Diagnosis And Repair

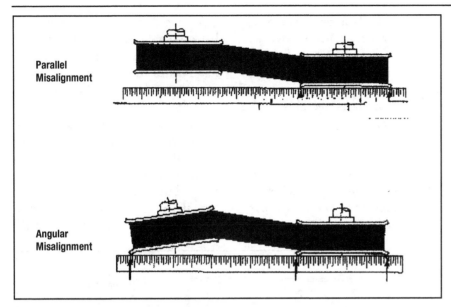

Two types of misalignment; parallel and angular.
(Courtesy: Gates Rubber Company)

drops as the voltage travels from the alternator to the battery. If a small voltage drop is detected, the alternator will boost the voltage to compensate. This helps to prolong battery life.

If there is no increase over the base reading, the charging system is inoperative and further tests will have to be performed. If an increase of over 2.0 volts occurs, a defective regulator, shorted components or a bad ground is indicated and further tests should be made.

If the voltage increase is not over 2.0 volts, a load test should be performed on the electrical system by using the vehicle's electrical components. With the components turned on, the voltage reading should be at a minimum of 1/2 volt above the base reading. This indicates that the alternator and regulator are functioning properly.

If a reading representing an increase between 0 and 2 volts is obtained, check the wiring between the alternator and batteries. Resistance anywhere in the wiring or connections will reduce the voltage and slow charging, even if the alternator is in good condition.

Throughout these tests, keep in mind that the voltage output of the alternator varies with both the load and the temperature. Maximum voltage will be produced only under light load and at relatively low temperatures. Higher temperatures and higher loads will reduce the charging voltage.

There is another critical point to consider on late-model heavy-duty trucks. Many of the latest diesel engines operate most efficiently at moderate cruising speeds, or when climbing hills. If this is the way the truck is being operated, there may be undercharge problems even though the alternator is functioning properly and its basic rating is correct for the application. The answer may be the installation of a different type of alternator designed to produce its output over a wider range of operating speeds, and with much less reduction in output at lower rpm.

CHARGING RATE

Insufficient charging can lead to poor starting performance and eventual battery failure. Overcharging leads to water loss and may cause the plates inside the battery to buckle due to excessive heat. Finding the correct charging rate is critical to good vehicle performance and long battery life.

Battery charging is affected by several key factors: the first is the difference between charging voltage and the post voltage of 12.6, and the second is time. In any situation where more time is available for charging, a lower voltage regulator setting is appropriate; in any situation where there are frequent starts and charging time is limited, a higher voltage regulator setting is appropriate.

Another variable is battery temperature. A cold battery will not provide full power; likewise, it will not rapidly accept a charge. In many applications that run in extreme cold, especially where there are frequent starts, a battery box heater may be needed to keep the batteries properly charged.

Similarly, a warm battery is more likely to be subject to overcharging. Alternators should have the appropriate voltage regulator settings when vehicles run consistently in a warm climate.

How do we know when battery-charging voltage is appropriate for the conditions? The answer is when the battery consistently remains at 90-95 percent of full charge.

BELTS, PULLEYS AND BRACKETS

Chirping noises from the engine compartment that increase in frequency as the engine rpm are raised can usually be attributed to belt squeal. Also, misalignment causes the belt span to enter the pulley on an angle, as initial contact is made with only one side of the belt. The greater this misalignment, the greater the vibration or chirping noise will be.

Angles between the belt span and the pulley are usually responsible for causing the 'chirp' associated

Charging System Diagnosis And Repair

with misalignment noise. This can be the result of different combination of pulley positions; parallel and angular being the most common.

Check the alternator belt(s) and any related components that may utilize the same belt(s) to see if they are functioning properly. If equipped, check the tensioner and its pulley for proper operation and alignment. While some tensioners are adjustable, others are spring loaded and designed to keep spring tension on the alternator belt. A weak spring will be evident when performing a belt deflection check.

Check the alternator belt(s) at the manufacturer's recommended intervals for evidence of wear such as cracking, fraying, missing sections, oil contamination and incorrect tension. Also, check for hard objects such as small stones or sand that may become imbedded in the bottom of the belt(s) or in the pulley grooves. Determine the belt tension at a point halfway between the pulleys by pressing on the belt with moderate thumb pressure. Compare belt deflection with manufacturer's specifications.

Inspect the alternator for looseness and improper alignment. An aligned pulley system reduces both pulley and belt wear, in addition to alternator vibration. If the belt pulleys are severely misaligned, look for improper positioning of the alternator due to missing, broken or loose mounting brackets, improper fit of the pulley or shaft, or even an incorrect alternator installed. Inspect the pulleys for chips, nicks, cracks, tool marks, bent sidewalls, severe corrosion or other damage. Parallel and angular pulley alignment can be checked with a straightedge.

NOTE: Depending on the specific engine, there is a possibility that other accessory drive belts may have to be removed before removing the alternator belt.

Loosen the belt tensioner or alternator pivot, and remove the belt. Never pry the belt from its pulley. After the belt is removed, spin the pulley to determine if there are any imperfections in the pulley or fan.

NOTE: On some vehicles, it is possible to replace the fan and pulley without removing the alternator, although this procedure is not recommended.

Always disconnect the negative battery cable before servicing the alternator. Next, remove the alternator wires. Loosen the mounting fasteners and remove the alternator assembly from the engine compartment. Mount the alternator on a workbench and use the appropriate tool(s) to remove the locking fastener from the front of the alternator. Then remove the pulley and fan. If the shaft is equipped with a keyway, make sure the woodruff

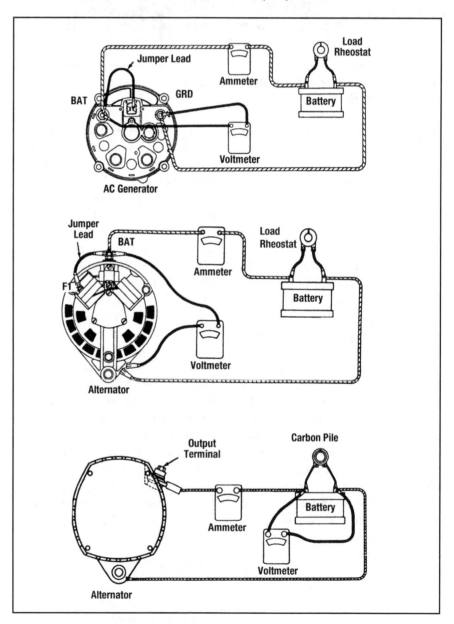

Testing alternator output using various methods. Connections may differ, but in most cases full battery voltage is applied to the alternator field in order to obtain maximum alternator output.

key does not get lost or damaged. Thoroughly inspect the alternator shaft and its keyway (if equipped) for damage.

NOTE: Make sure the replacement pulley and/or fan are proper for the application by comparing with manufacturer's recommendations. If the replacement fan is improperly sized, it may not cool the alternator efficiently. If the wrong sized pulley is used, belt adjustment will be difficult if not impossible, and alignment problems can occur.

Now, while the alternator is out of the engine compartment, inspect the mounting brackets again for looseness, bends, cracks and broken or missing parts. Most of the time it's easier to see any imperfections in the bracketry with the alternator removed. If any brackets are found to be damaged, repair as necessary. Inspect the tensioner pulley and make sure the bearings run smooth on the tensioner shaft. If the tensioner is bent or broken, or if the pulley is binding or making an abnormal noise, replace the tensioner assembly.

When installing the pulley and fan onto the alternator shaft, install the key into the slot on the shaft (if equipped) and properly mount the pulley and fan. Note that the open edges of the fan blades must be pointed toward the alternator. This ensures efficient air flow to the alternator assembly. Secure the assembly with the locking fastener and torque to manufacturer's specifications. Install the alternator assembly and reconnect the alternator wiring and negative battery cable.

Install a new belt by correctly positioning it in its pulley grooves. Using the proper tools, move the adjustment to tighten the belt, or in the case of automatically tensioned drives, move the tensioner to a position where the belt can be installed onto the pulleys. Use the proper tension recommendations for the particular application.

GEARS

While not as prevalent, some vehicles have a gear driven alternator that eliminates the need for a belt. Engine power is automatically transferred to the alternator via a gear mounted in back of the assembly. This gear is held in place by a woodruff key, nut and thrust washer, and is driven by a drive gear bolted to the crankshaft assembly.

To inspect and/or replace the gear, disconnect the negative battery cable and alternator wiring. Loosen the alternator fasteners and remove the alternator assembly from the vehicle.

Mount the alternator on a workbench and inspect the gear assembly. Rotate the shaft, looking for excessive play between the shaft and the gear. Inspect the gear teeth for damage or excessive wear. Inspect the crankshaft gear teeth for excessive damage or wear.

If the alternator gear must be removed for detailed inspection or replacement, remove the fastener and thrust washer, and slide the gear from the woodruff key and shaft. Make sure the woodruff key does not get lost or damaged, and inspect the keyway for wear. Closely inspect the gear for damage such as cracks, nicks, missing or chipped teeth, and keyway wear.

CAUTION: It is absolutely crucial that you use the manufacturer's-recommended replacement gear. Installing an improperly sized gear can damage the crankshaft drive gear.

Insert the woodruff key into the keyway and slide the gear onto the shaft, aligning it with the key. Install the thrust washer and nut, and torque the nut to manufacturer's specifications. Install the alternator while observing the gear alignment with the crankshaft gear. Install the fasteners and torque to manufacturer's specifications. Reconnect the alternator wiring and negative battery cable.

CHARGING SYSTEM VOLTAGE DROP

Excessive resistance in the voltage and/or ground sides of the charging circuit can cause a low charging rate due to the difference between alternator output and electrical system voltage requirements. Also, too much resistance in the ground system can actually fool the voltage regulator into increasing the voltage, resulting in an overcharging situation and premature battery failure. Charging system voltage drop is usually caused by a defective, incorrect or corroded cable from the alternator to the battery, or a poor ground connection on the negative side of the circuit.

To check for high resistance in the voltage side of the system, connect the DMM negative lead to the positive battery cable end. Next, connect the positive lead to the opposing cable end at the alternator. Read the voltage drop and compare with manufacturer's specifications. Normally, the voltage drop should not exceed 0.2 volts.

To check for high resistance in the ground side of the system, connect the DMM negative lead to the negative battery cable end. Next, connect the positive lead to the alternator grounding point (usually the alternator bracket). Read the voltage drop and compare with manufacturer's specifications. Normally, the voltage drop should not exceed 0.1 volt.

WIRES AND CONNECTORS

Good and proper wiring, along with clean, solid connections are

Charging System Diagnosis And Repair

a must. Without that, even the strongest alternator won't charge the system properly and failures will occur.

In today's vehicles, solid-state electronics depend so much on reliable wiring and connections that wire repair should be a secondary choice to replacement. However, in the event a repair is attempted, a high quality splice is generally an acceptable fix to remedy a problem. While some vendors maintain that shrink-wrap is for the most part, the sealant of choice, electrical tape can be a suitable equivalent; rosin core solder and splice clips definitely enhance the seal's durability.

Soldering irons are available in many sizes and wattage ratings. Irons with higher wattage deliver higher temperatures and recover lost heat faster. A soldering iron rated for no more than 50 watts is recommended, especially on electrical systems where excess heat can damage the components being soldered.

Three ingredients are necessary for successful soldering:
- Proper flux
- Good solder
- Sufficient heat.

Soldering flux is needed to clean the metal of tarnish, prepare it for soldering and enable the solder to spread into tiny crevices. Most solders contain a core of flux, therefore making separate fluxing unnecessary. Always check the solder to make sure it has a core of flux. If not, a separate soldering flux will be necessary.

Successful soldering requires that the metals to be joined be heated to a temperature that melts the solder, usually between 360° and 460°F. Contrary to popular belief, the purpose of the soldering iron is not to melt the solder itself, but to heat the components being soldered to a temperature high enough to melt the solder when it touches the work.

Soldering tips are made of copper for good heat conductivity, although they must be 'tinned' regularly for quick transfer of heat to the project and to prevent the solder from sticking to the iron. To tin the iron, heat it and touch the solder to the tip; the solder will flow over the hot tip. Wipe the excess off with a clean rag, using caution because the iron will be hot.

If possible, remove the component from the vehicle and place it on a wooden board. Using a metal work area can rob heat from the component to be soldered, which can make it difficult for the solder to melt. Firmly hold the work to be soldered and hold the soldering tip with the broadest face against the work. Use enough solder to give a heavy film between the iron and the piece being soldered, while moving slowly and making sure the solder melts properly. Keep the work level or the solder will run to the lowest part and favor the thicker parts.

NOTE: Don't let the soldering iron overheat. If it does, evidenced by burning of the solder on the face, it must be re-tinned.

Once the soldering is completed, let the soldered joint stand until cool to the touch. Use shrink wrap or electrical tape to seal the joint.

Terminal connectors pose their own threat to electrical conductivity. Check for loose or broken wire connections, and improperly formed or damaged terminals. All connector terminals in the circuit should be carefully inspected to determine the proper contact tension. Use a mating terminal to test contact tension. Ensure that all grounds are clean and making good contact. It is also important to make sure that water, dirt, and corrosion intrusion is kept at a minimum. A good quality electrical cleaning solution can be used to clean all contaminants from terminal connections.

Notes

Lighting Systems Diagnosis And Repair

INSPECTION

The lighting system on heavy-duty trucks can wreak havoc on the electrical system. The system's wiring proceeds from the power source to a circuit breaker, then to a switch and through a connector to the light assemblies. Periodically check to see that all wiring connections are clean and tight, that light units are tightly mounted to provide a good ground and that the headlights are properly adjusted. Loose or corroded connections can cause a discharged battery, difficult starting, dim lights and possible damage to the alternator or regulator.

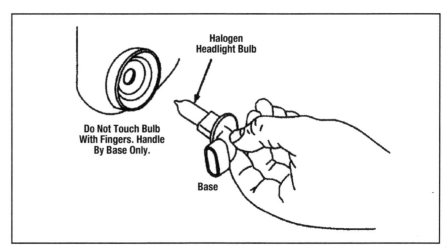

Never touch the glass of a quartz halogen composite bulb when servicing.

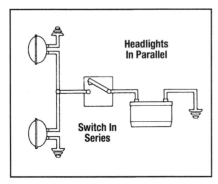

Headlamps are wired in parallel, thus providing more than one path for current flow. If one circuit is broken, the other light can remain operational as a complete circuit.

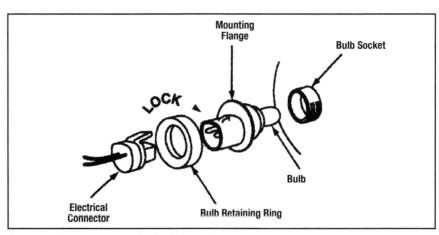

Quartz halogen composite bulb installation.

Lubricate sockets, pigtails, battery terminals and connections with a 'non-conductive' anti-corrosion compound. The purpose of the sealant is to protect against corrosion and water.

Wires and/or harnesses must be replaced if insulation becomes burned, cracked or deteriorated. Whenever it is necessary to splice a wire or repair one that is broken, use rosin flux solder to bond the splice and insulating tape to wrap all splices or bare wires. Do not attempt to make a splice by twisting the wire together and taping or by using wire nuts. These methods make poor connections that deteriorate quickly.

Make sure all exterior lights (including clearance lights) are working properly and secured to their mountings. Also, make sure all headlights are working in both low-and-high beam functions, and that headlight bulbs are not clouded or mounted improperly.

HEADLIGHTS

There are two basic types of headlight systems: the 2-light circuit and the 4-light circuit. Each system provides high and low beam functions. These lights are usually grounded, with the headlights and dimmer switches providing the power source.

In addition, there are two types of headlights: the traditional

Lighting Systems Diagnosis And Repair

sealed beam unit, or the now more prevalent quartz halogen composite unit. Practically all late model trucks use quartz-halogen composite headlights. In most cases, they almost double the candlepower and considerably enhance the distance a driver can see at night.

The filament in a composite light is contained in a pressurized gas environment, which allows the filament to be heated to higher temperatures. This produces a much brighter and whiter light, requiring less power than normal sealed beams.

It is important to keep in mind a few facts when servicing headlights:
- Keep the lens as clean as possible. This will allow the headlight to function as cool as possible
- Always use the appropriate lubricant on sockets, pigtails, battery terminals and connections
- Make sure all ground connections are clean and secure
- Always replace wiring, trailer light cables, and harnesses with an equal or heavier gauge wire
- Make sure all housings are secure and not damaged. Vibration can lead to premature bulb failure
- Never touch the glass of a quartz halogen composite bulb. Skin oils create hot spots on the bulb which in turn will cause the bulb to burn out prematurely
- Before performing lighting system tests, make sure the battery is in a fully-charged condition and all battery cable connections are clean and tight
- Check for wires with frayed or damaged insulation, loose connections and proper harness routing.

Use the following guidelines when checking the headlight system:

Headlights go dim
- Low battery charge
- Corrosion on sockets or connectors
- Low voltage output from charging system.

Headlights operate intermittently
- Loose connection(s) or wiring
- Poor ground
- Intermittent short circuit
- Defective headlight switch.

Headlights inoperative but parking lights work
- Open or shorted wiring
- Loose connections
- Defective dimmer switch
- Defective headlight switch.

In addition, if the headlights are brighter than normal, inspect the charging system voltage regulator for inappropriate voltage and repair as necessary. This problem can lead to premature headlight failure. Also, if one or more headlights are inoperative, check for defective bulbs, blown fuses, corroded light sockets, poor grounds or a defective headlight switch.

To replace a sealed beam unit, remove all trim that would impede the removal of the headlight. Remove the retainer ring fasteners and retainer ring from the headlight. Pull the sealed beam forward and disconnect the wire connector. Connect the wire connector to the replacement headlight and position the bulb in the housing. Reinstall the retainer ring along with the retainer screws. Reinstall all removed trim items. Check the headlight operation and aim if necessary.

Most quartz halogen composite bulbs can be replaced from behind the light assembly. Unscrew the bulb socket from the housing and withdraw the entire assembly from the light. Remove the old bulb from the socket, being careful not to touch the glass of the bulb. Install the replacement bulb and seat the socket-and-bulb assembly inside the light. Turn the socket to lock the assembly in place.

HEADLIGHT AIMING

Check that there is appropriate air in the tires, and align the headlights using a headlight adjustment tool, if necessary. This tool can be calibrated to accommodate a slight slope in the floor, making it usable in almost any surface in the shop as long as the floor is reasonably flat. Note that some headlight housings contain a bubble level to facilitate the alignment process.

Aiming consists of horizontally and vertically adjusting each headlight unit via adjusting screws, which move the retaining screws or headlight housing in the appropriate direction. There is no adjustment for focus.

HEADLIGHT SWITCH

The headlight switch on most vehicles operates the exterior lights and in some cases, the interior light circuits. Most headlight switches have a thermal circuit breaker built right into the switch itself. This breaker will cause the headlights to flash on and off if it overheats, which the manufacturers have deemed safer than having a fuse blow and losing all lights in darkness. Some models that do not use this thermal breaker design deploy separate fuses for right and left sides, or high and low beams, to avoid losing all lights at the same time.

In addition, some switches have a dual function. Instrument cluster brightening for twilight operation is the province of this second function, enabling the driver to adjust the brightness of the instrument cluster for easier visibility.

Lighting Systems Diagnosis And Repair

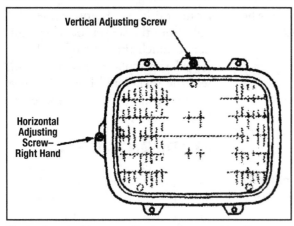

Typical sealed beam adjustment screw locations.

The headlight switch can be tested using a 12-volt test light along with a jumper wire and proper schematic or diagnostic flow chart. Follow the manufacturer's recommended procedure when testing the switch for proper voltage and continuity.

Consult the manufacturer's service manual for replacement since the headlight switch can be located in the dashboard or incorporated into the turn signal stalk as part of a combination or multifunction switch.

DIMMER SWITCH

Switching the headlight beams from low-to-high or from high-to-low is achieved by a dimmer switch, usually mounted on the steering column. This is usually combined with the turn signal switch, and can also be a part of the combination or multifunction switch. An indicator light, mounted on the dash panel, illuminates when the switch is in the high beam position. The combination or multifunction switch stalk may include other auxiliary system functions such as wipers, speed control, and headlights. Be careful, a short in the combination or multifunction switch can affect other vehicle systems too.

As with the headlight switch, the dimmer switch can be tested using a 12-volt test light along with a jumper wire and proper schematic or diagnostic flow chart. Follow the manufacturer's recommended procedure when testing the switch pins for proper voltage and continuity.

To replace the combination or multifunction switch remove the steering column cover and disconnect the steering column wiring connector from the switch. Remove the switch fasteners and switch assembly from the column.

NOTE: Some applications may require removal of the steering wheel in order to replace the combination or multifunction switch.

To install, reverse the removal procedure. After installation, check for proper operation.

DAYTIME RUNNING LIGHTS

Daytime running lights (DRL) are installed on some trucks. In this application, the headlights are illuminated when the ignition switch is turned ON. The DRL module also receives a signal from the vehicle speed sensor. As long as the vehicle is moving, the module keeps the headlights on. They are usually illuminated at 50% or less of normal intensity.

Always use the manufacturer's suggested procedures, voltages, and connector pin tests procedures when checking inoperative daytime running lights. Inspect the fuse, wires, and connectors.

Check for a voltage signal between the vehicle speed sensor and the DRL module. If voltage is not present, check for an open or short to ground in the circuit. If voltage is present, suspect a defective DRL module.

To replace the DRL module, locate and disconnect the wire harness from the module, and remove the module from its mounting.

PARKING, CLEARANCE AND TAILLIGHTS

The taillights, side markers, clearance, license plate light and front parking lights are usually on the same circuit as the headlights. The headlight switch controls their function, although some applications supply a separate switch for independent operation.

When the headlight switch is moved to the first position, these lights illuminate, while the headlights stay off. When the switch is moved to the second position, the lights illuminate along with the headlights. Any combination of these lights is available in standard incandescent, or the increasingly popular Light Emitting Diode (LED).

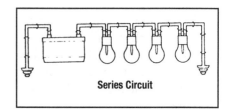

A series circuit provides only one path to ground. If series-connected bulbs were used, when one light burns out, they all will go out.

If only one light in a circuit is inoperative, visually check the bulb filament to see if it is broken or burned out. If the bulb is not defective, inspect the socket and wiring for damage or corrosion. If the bulb and socket are OK, check for an open in the wiring upstream from the light.

If all lights are inoperative, check the fuse or circuit breaker, and power supply. If no problem is found, check for an open in the circuit upstream from the light. If still no problem is found, perform a headlight switch test as per the manufacturer's instructions using a 12-volt test light, jumper wire and schematic.

INCANDESCENT LIGHTING

Incandescent bulbs use filaments that heat up and glow, thereby emitting light. The filament inside is extremely fragile, and subject to vibration. In addition, repeated on/off cycles will reduce the life span of an incandescent bulb. The advantage of incandescent bulbs is the ability of the bulb to cast light outward, which is a difficult task for the LED bulb.

Incandescent bulbs come in a variety of shapes and sizes, depending on the application. They are available in single or double contact. Power to the bulb can be checked using a 12-volt test light. Always check for corroded light sockets, damaged wiring and poor grounds.

Single contact bulbs have only one filament and are found on lights that only have one function, on or off. Double contact bulbs have two filaments and are found on lights that have a dual function, such as turn signals and parking lights. These bulbs have index pins on each side in order to lock the bulb into the socket. Single contact bulbs have pins that are directly opposite each other, while double contact bulbs have staggered indexing lugs.

In either case, replacement consists of removing the lens from the front or removing the bulb socket from the rear, and twisting the bulb counterclockwise while pushing down slightly to unlock the pins.

LED LIGHTING

Light Emitting Diodes (LED) bulbs operate on a different concept than incandescent bulbs. Instead of using the fragile filament, the LED is solid state, utilizing an electronic chip in epoxy substrate. Because of this, durability and protection is increased, and maintenance hassles are reduced.

Although LEDs are visibly brighter than incandescent bulbs, they do not cast most of their light outward. Instead, the light is mostly confined within the bulb area, making the bulb itself more visible. LEDs also consume up to 90 percent less power than incandescent bulbs, helping to reduce the load on electrical systems and extend battery life. This limited current draw is also sought after by manufacturers, as more and more electronics are introduced into vehicles.

LEDs can remain effective for up to 100,000 hours, while their incandescent counterparts may remain effective from 200 to 15,000 hours, depending upon the size of the bulb and conditions in which the bulb is exposed. In addition, LED on-time response is quicker, which can be safer for both operators and motorists.

The drawbacks to LED lighting are the initial price, and the fact that if a multiple light unit is subject to one or more bulb failures, the entire unit must be replaced. This is a rare occurrence, however

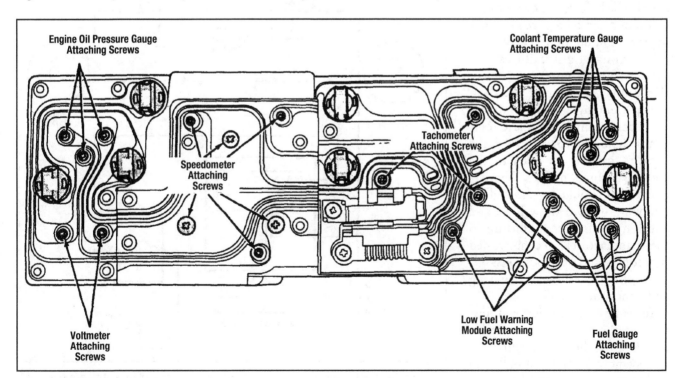

Typical printed circuit. (Courtesy: Ford Motor Co.)

Lighting Systems Diagnosis And Repair

it does happen occasionally. Also, because of the limited current draw, LED lamps are susceptible to snow and ice buildup as they do not generate as much heat.

LEDs are now available in single and double contact for applications such as clearance, stop, tail and turn signals. This eliminates the necessity of replacing the entire light assembly when switching from incandescent to LED.

DASH LIGHTS

Dash lights enable the driver to see all functions on the dash such as the speedometer, tachometer, air gauges, etc. Although often overlooked, these lights are an important factor in the safe operation of the vehicle.

Dash lights are usually the wedge type push-in bulbs, which can be accessed from behind the dash. Special sockets that make contact with the printed circuit board are mounted into the board in back of the dash. The socket is removed by twisting it and releasing it from the board. The bulb comes out with the socket and can be replaced by pulling it straight out from the socket.

Individual light failures can usually be attributed to a defective bulb. However, if the dash is experiencing multiple failures on a consistent basis, the circuit board should be checked for loose circuits, causing an open to the particular component(s). The circuit board should be checked by removing it from the vehicle and checking resistance according to the manufacturer's recommended procedures and specifications. Always check for damaged wiring and poor connections.

To remove the circuit board, disconnect the negative battery cable and remove the instrument cluster assembly. Remove all bulb and socket assemblies from the board. Loosen the fasteners and remove the printed circuit from the instrument cluster. To install, reverse the removal procedure.

FIBER OPTIC LIGHTING

Some trucks are equipped with fiber optic lighting in order to transmit light along great distances using one single light source. This is done by way of fiber optic cable. Fiber optic cable is made up of thousands of tiny, flexible glass strands, which carry light reflections along the inner core of the cable. An outer core that helps to contain the light reflection wraps the inner core. If the outer core is damaged, light will escape at the damaged point, thus rendering the light ineffective.

Optical fibers are lighter than normal wiring, and instead of transmitting an electrical signal to operate a light; in most cases they carry the actual light itself. Light sources can be placed in convenient locations to allow for better servicing. For example, a light source can be centrally located to avoid disassembly of an entire dash in order to repair instrument panel lights. Using fiber optics also reduces the heat that incandescent light bulbs produce.

NOTE: Some fiber optics use transducers to change electrical signals to light pulse signals. These light pulse signals are reflected along the fiber optic cable, and once they reach their destination, another transducer changes the light pulse back to an electrical signal.

INTERIOR LIGHTS

Various switches in the cab and sleeper can operate interior lights. Switches in the door jamb control

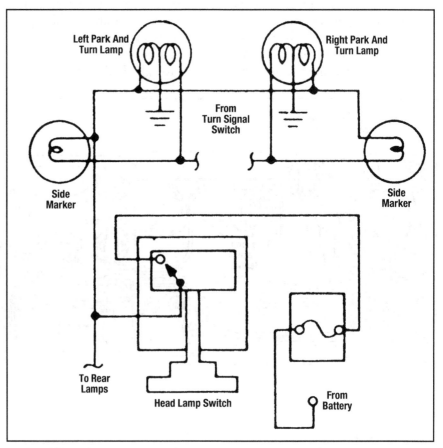

Side marker lights, taillights, parking lights and license plate lights are usually located on the same circuit.

Lighting Systems Diagnosis And Repair

some interior lights so that when the doors are opened, the lights will light. Courtesy light circuits may include the storage areas, map lights and instrument panel, with separate switches to control their operation.

Open and close the driver and passenger doors separately, noting interior light operation. Note that some vehicles may have a master override switch for this function. Make sure the switch is in the ON position. Operate the dash, map, sleeper and storage compartment lights to make sure they are working properly.

If the interior lights illuminate when one door is opened but not the other, suspect a defective or damaged door switch. If all interior lights are inoperative, check for a blown fuse. If the fuse is OK, suspect a defective master switch. If one or more interior lights are inoperative, remove the lens or socket assembly and check for power to the light. If there is power, replace the bulb assembly. If there is no power, check for a problem in the circuit such as a corroded light socket, damaged wire, poor connections, or ineffective ground. Repair as necessary.

STOP, TURN, HAZARD AND BACK-UP LIGHTS

These lights are undoubtedly the most important on the exterior of the vehicle because while other lights (such as headlights and parking lights) enable the driver to see and be seen, these lights tell surrounding motorists what the driver's intentions are while the vehicle is in operation. While the majority of these lights are equipped with incandescent bulbs, some are equipped with LEDs.

STOPLIGHTS

The stoplight switch is located on or near the brake pedal arm, so that it can be activated by depressing the brake pedal assembly. On vehicles with air brakes, the switch is an electro-pneumatic, non-grounded switch that operates in tandem with a two-way check valve. When the brakes are applied, the air pressure moves an internal switch that completes the circuit, activating the stoplights.

To check the switch, check for voltage at the electrical connection. If there is no voltage, check the fuse and wiring. If voltage is present, install an air gauge in the service line and gradually apply the brakes. The stoplights should illuminate at 6 psi or less. Check for air leaks at the switch. No air leaks are permissible.

On vehicles with hydraulic brakes, the stoplight switch maintains contact with the pedal arm, and when activated, closes the stoplight circuit. Check for voltage at the switch. If there is no voltage, check the fuse and wiring. If voltage is present, activate the switch and check for voltage on the opposite side of the switch. If voltage is not present, replace the switch assembly. If voltage is present, check the wiring, bulbs and connections in the stoplight circuit downstream of the stoplight switch and repair as necessary.

TURN SIGNALS, HAZARD AND BACK-UP LIGHTS

Turn the ignition key to the ON position, and operate the turn signals. Make sure the lenses are intact and clear. The flashing speed is dependent upon the wattage or load on the bulbs.

NOTE: Many newer vehicles use solid-state lighting control modules in place of flashers to control the function of the turn signals and four-way hazards, as well as other lighting functions.

The turn signal or combination/multifunction switch is located on the left side of the steering column, and is composed of a variety of off/on switches packaged as a single unit. To check the switch, use a 12-volt test light to see if there is voltage at the feed side of the switch. If voltage is not present, check the fuse and wiring upstream of the switch. If voltage is present, activate the switch and check for voltage at the flasher. If voltage is present, replace the flasher. If voltage is not present, check the wiring and connections between the

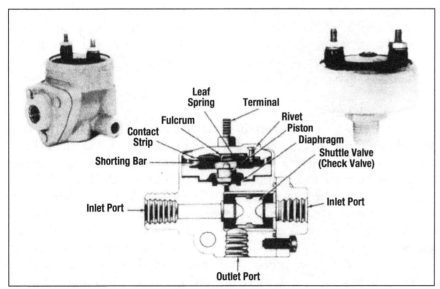

Stoplight switch and double check valve on vehicle with air brakes.
(Courtesy: Bendix Commercial Vehicle Systems)

Lighting Systems Diagnosis And Repair

switch and flasher. If the wiring is OK, replace the turn signal switch.

If there are still no turn signals after you've checked the turn signal switch and flasher operation, check the wiring, bulbs and connections in the circuit downstream from the flasher and repair as necessary.

To replace the turn signal or combination switch, remove the steering column cover and disconnect the steering column wiring connector from the switch. Remove the switch fasteners and switch assembly from the column. Some applications may require removal of the steering wheel in order to replace the combination switch.

WARNING: *If the vehicle is equipped with an inflatable Supplemental Restraint System (SRS) air bag, disarm the system according to manufacturer's procedures before removing the steering wheel.*

To install, reverse the removal procedure. After installation, check for proper operation.

The hazard system operates independently of the turn signals. All turn signal lights can be made to flash at the same time by activating the switch. To check the switch, use a 12-volt test light to see if there is voltage at the feed side of the switch. If voltage is not present, check the fuse, connections and wiring upstream from the switch and repair as necessary. If voltage is present, activate the switch and check for voltage at the flasher. If voltage is present, replace the flasher. If voltage is not present, check the wiring between the switch and flasher and repair as necessary. If the wiring is OK, replace the hazard switch.

If there are still no hazard lights after you've checked the hazard switch and flasher operation, check the wiring, bulbs and connections

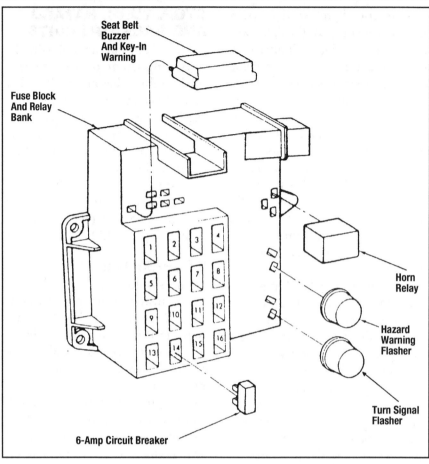

Hazard flashers and turn signal flashers look alike, but when switched, a change in the flashing rate will result.

in the circuit downstream from the flasher and repair as necessary.

NOTE: *Most vehicles use separate turn signal and hazard flasher circuits. Therefore, a regular turn signal flasher can't be used for a hazard flasher because the additional load would result in rapid flashing.*

Hazard switches can be located on the steering column or dash, depending on the application, and can be simply removed by disconnecting the wire connector and removing the switch from its mounting. Note that on some vehicles, certain dash components must be removed to gain access to the hazard switch and/or its connection.

Flasher locations vary from vehicle to vehicle. Usually, they're located behind the dash on the left side. However, some flasher units for the turn signal and hazard flasher systems are located in the fuse panel itself. They can be removed by simply pulling them straight out from the plug. When installing a new flasher, line up the metal contacts with the slots in the plug, and then press the flasher firmly into place.

Place the shifter control in reverse and check back-up light operation. White back up lights light up when the current is provided via the ignition switch. The switch for the back-up lights is mounted on the transmission or shift linkage.

Turn the ignition key to the ON position. Make sure the lenses are intact and clear. Block the wheels and place the shifter in reverse. Check for power at the feed side of the back-up light switch. If there

44   T6 - Electrical/Electronic Systems

Lighting Systems Diagnosis And Repair

is no power, check the fuse. If the fuse is OK, check the wiring and connections upstream from the switch. If there is power, check for voltage on the opposite side of the switch. If there is no voltage, replace the switch.

NOTE: If the power supply or switch is defective, it will affect both back-up lights.

If there are still no back-up lights after you've checked the switch, check the wiring, bulbs and connections in the circuit downstream from the switch and repair as necessary.

Some vehicles come equipped with a back-up alarm that is connected to the back-up light circuit and sounds when the transmission is placed in reverse. Its primary function is to alert people behind the vehicle that it is backing up.

With the key switch in the ON position (engine off), check for power at the feed side of the alarm. If there is power, the alarm should be sounding. If there is no power, check the wiring and connections in the circuit upstream from the alarm and repair as necessary. Also, make sure the alarm is properly adjusted and grounded. Most back-up alarms are audibly adjustable, with a volume switch on the alarm to control the loudness of the signal.

TRAILER LIGHT CORD AND PLUG

Be sure to check the trailer circuit connector, better known as a "light cord plug." The wiring connector is located behind the cab, directly behind the driver. A seven-wire core leads from the connector to the trailer, where it branches out to the various trailer lights. The standardized wire colors are given in the following table:

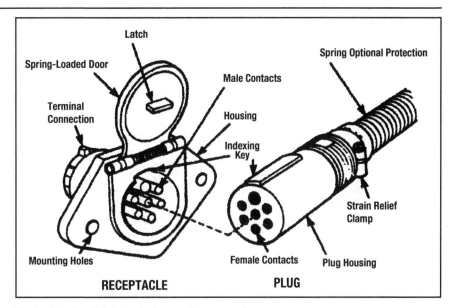

Typical trailer light cord plug and receptacle.

Wire Color	Light and Signal Circuits
White	Ground return to towing vehicle
Black	Clearance, side marker & ID lights
Yellow	Left-hand turn signal and hazard signal
Red	Stoplights and anti-wheel lock devices
Green	Right-hand turn signal and hazard signal
Brown	Tail and license plate lights
Blue	Auxiliary circuit

Testing of the connector can be performed by either a seven-pin plug tester or by a DMM using the manufacturer's recommended procedure. Voltage must be present at the plug circuits when the specific lights are activated inside the cab. If voltage is not present, check the fuse related to the particular circuit. If the fuse is OK, check for proper voltage in particular light circuit switches, wiring and connections and make repairs as necessary.

Notes

Related Vehicle Systems Diagnosis And Repair

INSTRUMENT CLUSTERS

Several different types of displays are used for electronic instrumentation. They include Light Emitting Diode (LED), Liquid Crystal Display (LCD), Vacuum Tube Fluorescent (VTF) and Cathode Ray Tube (CRT), and in some cases fiber optics.

LED displays, when used in instrument clusters are usually red, yellow or green in color. A typical LED requires about 35 milliamps for each segment to light.

LCD displays are used to form numbers, letters or symbols. They consist of liquid, sandwiched between two polarized sheets of glass. The liquid will permit light to pass through if a small voltage is applied.

A CRT cluster is basically a television tube or computer screen. This display's functions are controlled the same way as those of personal computers.

VTF also works in a fashion similar to CRT. VTF displays are very bright and are usually green in color. The electronics necessary for this type of instrument are very complex, and similar to those of a radio or television.

Electronic instrument panels operate from the same sender singles. For example, a sending unit from a fuel tank may vary from 0 (zero) ohms (empty) to 100 ohms (full). A digital dash using a 20-segment display would decrease one segment for every 5 ohms change.

Besides replacement, there is little that can be done to repair most digital instrument panels. Checking for proper changes from the sender(s) can determine if the problem is located in the sender or wiring, or if the problem is in the instrument display.

BIMETAL DASH GAUGES

Bimetal gauges employ a bimetallic strip to sense current flow. The two metals, which make up the strip, expand at different rates. Therefore, as the temperature of the strip changes, the metals work against each other and make the strip bend back-and-forth. The free end of the strip operates the gauge needle through a simple linkage.

Where a bimetal gauge is used to read fuel level, the sending unit located in the tank consists of a resistor and a sliding contact. A float determines the position of the contact. As the sliding contact moves across the resistor, current is sent in varying amounts to either the gauge or ground.

Some dashboards use a voltage regulator to supply a constant 3 volts to all the dash gauges. In cases where all the gauges develop similar problems all at the same time, the voltage regulator is at fault.

THERMAL ELECTRIC GAUGES

In thermal electric gauge installations, electricity comes from the ignition switch to one side of the gauge. It then goes through the gauge and on to the sending unit, which provides the necessary ground. Thermal electric gauges can be easily identified because the gauge needles return to the zero reading when the ignition switch is in the OFF position.

Thermal electric gauges pass current through a bimetal strip. One side of the strip heats faster than the other side, causing the strip to bend and move the pointer of the gauge.

MAGNETIC DASH GAUGES

Magnetic gauges use two electromagnetic coils of different sizes to influence the location of the gauge pointer. The smaller coil receives a constant supply of current directly from the ignition switch at all times and tends to pull the needle downscale. The larger coil receives all of the current passing through the unit and to ground when full-scale readings are required.

Under all other circumstances, varying amounts of current are passed through the sending unit to ground. When less than full current passes through the larger coil, the smaller coil tends to pull the pointer part way over toward the low side of the scale.

Magnetic gauges can suffer from improper supply voltage to the gauge. This is likely if there is no response from the gauge when the sending unit terminal is grounded. Test for voltage at the ignition switch terminal of the gauge and correct any problems. If there is voltage here and the gauge fails to respond, replace it.

If the ignition switch is defective, there will also be problems with the gauges. If there is no voltage to the gauge, but there is voltage at the ignition switch accessory terminal, check the wire supplying voltage to the gauge.

WARNING SYSTEMS

Warning signals receive voltage whenever the ignition switch is turned on. The circuit is completed to ground whenever the sending unit contacts close, allowing current to flow through the light and/or buzzer.

Related Vehicle Systems Diagnosis And Repair

Oil pressure signals activate when a diaphragm-operated switch senses less than a minimum level of oil pressure. Coolant temperature signals are energized when a bimetal element closes the contacts in the sending unit at a predetermined, maximum, safe operating temperature.

If the light or buzzer is on all the time, disconnect the connection at the sending unit. If the light or alarm stays on, the problem is a ground between the light or buzzer and sending unit. Replace the wire connecting the two or repair it where it may be grounded.

If the warning goes off when the wire is disconnected, the problem is most likely to be in the sending unit. The oil pressure unit performance can be checked by removing the unit and installing a gauge to make sure there is adequate oil pressure. If the pressure meets specifications and the light still stays on all of the time, replace the sending unit.

For temperature warning, it will be obvious that the sending unit is defective if the warning system activates even when the engine is cold, but disconnecting the connector at the unit causes the warning system to go off. If the system comes on when the engine is at operating temperature, be aware that there are several other potential causes of the problem. It is important to verify that all elements in the cooling system are in proper working condition.

If the warning system fails to work when there are engine problems, disconnect the wire at the sending unit and ground it. If this causes the system to operate, replace the sending unit. Note that temperature warning depends upon both sufficient antifreeze strength and radiator pressure. Check these before replacing a sending unit that fails to illuminate the light.

If there is still no response, check for voltage at the positive terminal of the light socket or warning buzzer and at the ignition switch accessory terminal. If there is no voltage, replace the switch. If the voltage is reaching the light socket or buzzer, ground the socket or buzzer at the ground terminal. If this causes the light or buzzer to operate, repair the wire connecting the light socket to the sending unit. Otherwise, replace the light or buzzer.

SENSORS

Engine Oil Pressure

The engine oil pressure sensor monitors engine oil pressure to warn of failures in the lubrication system. This sensor contains a pressure-sensitive diaphragm and an electrical amplifier. Mechanical pressure applied to the diaphragm causes the diaphragm to deflect, causing the amplifier to produce an electrical signal proportional to the deflection. This signal is sent to the oil pressure gauge.

NOTE: It's a good idea to test the oil pressure at the engine before diagnosing the gauge circuit.

Disconnect the wire from the sending unit and connect a variable resistance between the end of the wire and a good ground. Turn the ignition switch to the ON position and adjust the resistance. This should make the gauge move. If the gauge does not move, check for problems in the wiring; if the wiring is OK, suspect a defective gauge. If the gauge moves, suspect a defective sending unit.

Temperature

The coolant temperature sensor changes resistance as the coolant temperature changes. The sensor's output is monitored by the electronic control module (ECM), and in the case of electronically controlled engines, regulates various engine control functions. As the electrical resistance changes, it is displayed on the dash gauge as a temperature reading.

If the cooling system is deemed to be in proper working order, remove the wire from the sending unit on the engine and connect a variable resistance between the end of the wire and a good ground. With the ignition switch in the ON position, adjusting the resistance should make the gauge read through the full range.

If there is no movement of the gauge, it is either defective or not receiving current. If the gauge moves, suspect a defective sending unit.

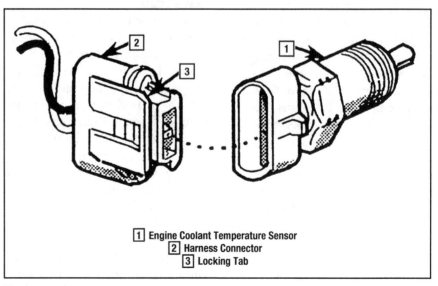

[1] Engine Coolant Temperature Sensor
[2] Harness Connector
[3] Locking Tab

Engine coolant temperature sensor.

Related Vehicle Systems Diagnosis And Repair

Fuel

Located in the fuel tank, the fuel-sending unit consists of a float, usually made of foam, connected by a metal rod mounted to a variable resistor. Progressively resistant material runs along a strip, which is connected, to a ground on one side. As the fuel level fluctuates, the up-or-down movement of the float pushes the contact along the strip, thereby increasing or decreasing resistance. This in turn controls the voltage to the gauge to accurately display the amount of fuel in the tank.

To test the sending unit, remove the wire connector from the unit and remove the unit from the tank. Use a DMM to check resistance while moving the float arm back-and-forth. Compare resistance measurements against manufacturer's specifications. If the readings are incorrect, replace the unit.

A fuel gauge should move toward full if the wire to the sender is disconnected. Reconnecting the wire, thereby lowering resistance, should cause the gauge to move smoothly toward empty. This is typical of most types of instrument gauge operation.

Also, fuel gauges may be tested using a known good spare sending unit. Disconnect the wire from the vehicle's sending unit and connect it to the spare unit. Ground the unit to the frame with a jumper wire and turn the ignition switch to the ON position. Move the unit through its full range. The dash gauge should operate through its own full range. If it does, the problem is in the vehicle's sending unit. If the gauge will not work, use a DMM to check for voltage and resistance in the wiring and dash gauge following manufacturer's procedures and specifications.

Electronic Speedometer

A vehicle speed sensor mounted in the transmission case produces a signal that varies in frequency as the transmission output shaft rotates. Mounted on the output shaft is a magnetic coil pickup. As the shaft rotates, the frequency of the pickup sends a pulse signal to the ECM, which in turn sends the signal to the electronic speedometer. As the vehicle accelerates or decelerates, the output shaft speed changes, thereby changing the frequency of the signal to the speedometer. In addition to speedometer operation, the speed sensor is designed to monitor vehicle speed for items such as the odometer, tachometer, ABS, traction control and cruise control.

Today's electronic speedometers have a self-calibration transducer that takes the guesswork out of calibration issues. However, if the vehicle has an earlier style electronic speedometer, or if the vehicle's drivetrain components have been altered (different size tires, wheelbase changes, etc.), the speedometer must be calibrated.

The easiest way to check the speedometer calibration is by driving. First, inspect and adjust all fluid levels and check for proper tire/wheel installation and matching. Make sure the tires are properly inflated.

Drive the vehicle at 60 mph for a measured one-mile stretch while using a stopwatch to time the interval. It should take 60 seconds to travel the mile. If the timing is off, the speedometer must be calibrated according to manufacturer's procedures and specifications.

In addition, a properly calibrated dynamometer can also be used to check calibration. Drive the vehicle onto the dynamometer and install safety chains, straps and/or wheel chocks. Install the appropriate instrumentation to the vehicle's serial communications port.

Make sure all electrical accessories are off, and all accessories such as PTOs are disengaged. Start the engine and allow it to warm up to operating temperature. Engage the dynamometer and increase engine load until the engine and drivetrain are at operating temperature. After warm-up, all engine accessories except the cooling fan should be operating at minimum levels, and the brake system air pressure (if equipped) should be at normal operating levels.

Place or lock the transmission in direct drive and run to test speeds as required by the manufacturer, noting test data. After the test has been completed, removed all testing instrumentation, disengage the cooling fan, disconnect all safety chains, and remove wheel tie-down straps or chocks.

Depending on the particular application, speedometer calibration may consist of replacing the vehicle speed sensor or using a commercially available speed sensor calibrator. Install the calibrator into the existing wiring and drive the vehicle over a measured distance. Note the odometer reading. Using the calibrator instructions, adjust the switches and retest the vehicle over the same distance.

Horn

WARNING: If the vehicle is equipped with an inflatable Supplemental Restraint System (SRS) air bag, disarm the system according to manufacturer's procedures before servicing the horn button or wiring.

Typically, the electric horn is activated by a relay in the horn circuit. When a relay is used in a horn circuit, the electromagnetic coil of the relay is energized by a controlled amount of current when the horn button is depressed, grounding the circuit. As the magnetic field is produced in the coil, a set of points is closed between the battery and the horns, completing the circuit and allowing a greater amount of current flow. When the horn button is released, the magnetic field is stopped. The points then open and stop current flow to the horn.

Related Vehicle Systems Diagnosis And Repair

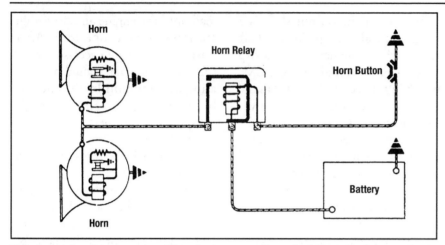

This horn circuit has a relay. The electromagnetic coil of the relay is energized by a controlled amount of current via the horn button.

Most horn problems can be linked to wiring problems in the control or power feed circuit, the relay or the switch. However, some horns are adjustable. Try to adjust the horns before replacing them. The adjusting screw is usually found on the horn body assembly.

The screw should be turned in either direction until the horn sounds correctly. The adjustment screw should be set at the point where the horn current draw is between 4 and 6.5 amperes. Amperage should be measured in series or with an inductive pickup meter around the horn power feed wire.

To diagnose the cause of a malfunctioning horn, supply a good ground to the switch terminal at the relay. If the horn sounds, suspect a problem in the ground and/or horn button circuit.

The horn chassis ground can be checked by connecting a jumper wire from the horn's frame to a good body ground. If the horn sounds when the horn button is pressed, the horn chassis ground should be serviced.

If the horn does not sound, check for voltage at the relay coil and at the breaker connection in the horn relay. If voltage is present, use a jumper wire to connect the battery feed to the horn. If the horn sounds, suspect a problem with the relay. If no voltage is present at the relay, check the fuse and connecting wires and/or harness.

If the horn sound is a low-pitched moan, the current is probably too high. Adjust the horn using the previously discussed procedure. If the horn sound is weak, current is probably too low; suspect poor electrical connections. If the horn tone is too harsh, it is possible the horn body is contacting the vehicle's sheet metal.

Continuous horn sounding usually indicates a stuck horn switch or relay contacts. To determine the cause, disconnect the relay and check for continuity across the horn feed contacts. If there is continuity, the relay contacts are stuck and the relay should be replaced. If there is no continuity between the contacts, check the horn button assembly.

Wipers And Washers

A multi-speed motor, the speeds of which are typically controlled by a resistor, powers the windshield wipers on most vehicles. The resistor changes the amount of current that flows through the field windings of the motor assembly. A set of gears, crank arm and the necessary linkage are used to connect the windshield wiper motor to the wipers.

Depending on the particular vehicle, there may be one or more relays either underneath the dash or in the engine compartment, so it's a good idea to have a wiring schematic and diagnostic trouble tree. It could save hours of troubleshooting if you are aware of all the components in the particular system.

Intermittent wipers use a variable resistor to control the current to a pause control module or wiper relay. The wiper motor is connected directly to the pause module or relay, and when current is interrupted, the wipers move to the parked position. The variable resistor controls how long the wipers will be off. The greater the current flow to the module, the less time the wipers will be off.

On some vehicles, the windshield washer pump is located on the wiper motor gearbox, and is driven by the wiper motor. When the washer switch is activated, a relay coil provides for the connection between the motor and the pump. Other systems are equipped with a separate motorized washer pump located in the bottom of the washer fluid reservoir or near the wiper motor assembly.

Identifying the cause of malfunctioning wiper systems may be difficult because the problem may be electrical or mechanical. As a starting point, disconnect the linkage from the motor. If the motor turns after the switch is turned on, the linkage may be binding. Check the linkage and bushings and replace as necessary. If the motor does not run, suspect the motor or an electrical problem in the wiper circuit.

To diagnose electrical problems, begin by checking the fuse. If the fuse is OK, check and clean the motor's mounting and ground connections. Visually inspect all electrical connections to the motor. Since each manufacturer and model uses different approaches to wiper circuit design, use a schematic of the circuit and diagnostic flow chart.

With the ignition and wiper control switch on, test for voltage at the motor. If voltage is present, suspect

Related Vehicle Systems Diagnosis And Repair

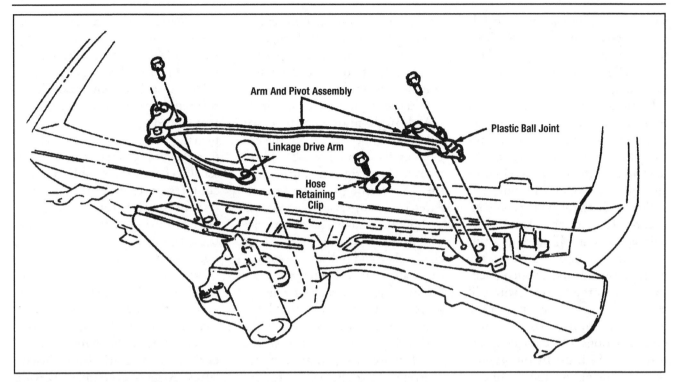

Windshield wiper pivot shaft and linkage assembly removal. *(Courtesy: Ford Motor Company)*

the motor. If no voltage is present, check for voltage at the battery side of the switch. If voltage is present there, replace the switch. If no voltage is present, check the circuit from the fuse to the switch.

When the washer system is inoperative, first check the fluid level and refill if necessary. If there is an ample amount of fluid, disconnect the hose from the pump to the nozzles, and operate the washer switch. If fluid comes out of the pump, check the hose for kinks, blockages and proper routing and make sure the nozzles are clear. If fluid does not come out of the pump, the problem is the pump or its power feed circuit. Check for voltage to the pump when the switch is activated. If voltage is present, suspect the pump. If no voltage is found, check the pump power feed circuit wiring, connections and relay (if equipped).

Power Mirrors

Motorized side view mirrors are available in some vehicles in order to ease adjustability for the driver. They can also be an aid to the driver when maneuvering the vehicle into tight spaces. The electrically powered mirror is powered by a servo motor inside the mirror head, and can be serviced separately. The control switch(es) are located inside the cab within reach of the driver. Usually, one part of the control switch allows for selection of either the right-hand or left-hand mirror, and another part allows for the adjustment of the mirror position.

If both mirrors are inoperative, first check the fuse. If the fuse is OK, remove the door or dash panel trim to gain access to the back of the switch, and check for power at the feed side of the switch using a 12-volt test light. If there is no power at the switch, check the wiring and connections between the fuse panel and the switch and repair as necessary. If there is power to the switch, use a jumper wire across the appropriate switch circuits as described by the manufacturer. If the mirrors can be operated, replace the switch.

If a single mirror is inoperative, verify that the harness is connected to the servo motor. Using a 12-volt test light, check for power in the harness connector at the servo motor by operating the switch. If there is power and the mirror is inoperative, replace the servo motor. If there is no power, check the wiring and connections back to the switch and repair as necessary.

Some mirrors are heated to aid in the process of defrosting and demisting in cold, damp climates. Heated mirror controls are completely separate from the power mirror control circuit, and may include a thermo-switch to allow current to flow to the mirror heating element when outside ambient temperatures are at a specified point.

If you suspect no voltage to the heated mirrors evidenced by both elements being inoperative, first check the fuse. If the fuse is OK, check for power at the feed side of the switch using a 12-volt test light. If there is no power at the switch, check the wiring and connections between the fuse panel and the switch and repair as necessary. If there is power to the switch, check for power on the opposite side of the switch after it is activated. If there is no power, replace the switch.

If you suspect one heating element to be inoperative, use the manufacturer's procedure to remove the mirror glass. Check for power at the feed side of the thermo-switch or element terminal. If no power is available, check the wiring and connections back to the switch and repair as necessary. If power is available, connect an ohmmeter to the mirror terminals and a hot/cold sensor tester to the thermo-switch (if equipped). Lower the temperature of the tester to manufacturer's recommendations. Once the temperature is reached, the thermo-switch should close and/or the ohmmeter should show specific resistance according to manufacturer's specifications. If resistance is normal, replace the heating element.

AC COMPRESSOR CLUTCH

One thing all modern A/C compressors have in common is a coil and clutch. The electromagnetic clutch provides the mechanical link between the pulley and compressor.

A stationary electromagnetic coil is attached to the face of the compressor behind the pulley. When current flows through the coil windings, a magnetic field pulls the drive hub snug against the pulley. Now functioning as a single unit, they drive the compressor as long as the coil is energized. Based on demand from the thermostatic controls, power is switched on or off to the clutch coil.

If after verifying system pressure, the compressor does not run, use a DMM to check to see if the clutch is getting power. Also, check to see if the compressor is properly grounded. If the compressor is not getting power, apply 12 volts to the power connector to see if the clutch will function. If the clutch engages, the problem is in the compressor power circuit. If the compressor clutch does not engage, suspect a defective compressor clutch coil.

Although many compressor clutches can be serviced in the engine compartment, it is advisable to recover the refrigerant and remove the compressor from the vehicle. After the compressor is removed, clamp it in a suitable holding device with the clutch facing upward. If the clutch plate and hub are fastened to the shaft using a retainer such as a C-clip, remove the clip using the appropriate removal tool. If the clutch plate and hub are fastened to the shaft using a bolt or nut, hold the clutch plate using an appropriate clutch plate holding tool and remove the bolt or nut with a socket wrench.

After the retainer has been removed, attach a clutch plate and hub puller into the hub assembly. Using the appropriate wrenches, turn the center screw of the puller into the puller body until the clutch plate and hub have been separated from the shaft. Remove the Woodruff key from the hub and place it aside for future use.

To remove the clutch rotor assembly, remove the rotor and bearing retaining ring, and install the appropriate puller. Hold the puller in place and tighten the puller screw against the guide to remove the pulley rotor and bearing assembly.

Next, remove the clutch coil by installing the appropriate puller on the front head of the compressor. Tighten the forcing screw against the puller pilot to remove the coil assembly.

When installing the coil, place the assembly on the front head of the compressor with the terminals in the proper position. Place a suitable installation tool over the opening of the clutch coil housing and align the installer with the compressor front head. Turn the installation tool forcing screw to force the clutch coil onto the front head until it is properly seated. Make sure the installation tool is properly aligned during installation.

Now, install the compressor clutch rotor and bearing assembly on the front head. Position a rotor and bearing installation tool directly over the rotor and tighten the center screw to force the assembly onto the compressor front head. Make sure the installation tool is properly aligned during installation. Once the assembly is properly seated, install the retainer ring.

When installing the replacement clutch and hub, place the Woodruff key into the hub groove. Make sure that the frictional surfaces of the clutch plate and clutch rotor are free of dirt, oil and debris before installation. Align the shaft keyway with the Woodruff key and place the clutch plate and hub assembly onto the compressor shaft.

CAUTION: Do not drive or pound on the clutch hub or shaft. Internal damage to the compressor can result.

Using a clutch plate and hub installation tool, press the hub onto the shaft. Tighten the body several turns and remove the installation tool. This is to make sure that the Woodruff key is still in place in the keyway, before installing the clutch plate and hub assembly into its final position. After the clutch plate and hub have been seated, check the air gap between the frictional surfaces against manufacturer's specifications.

If the air gap is sufficient, remove the installation tool, and double-check for proper Woodruff key positioning. If the retainer is a C-clip, install the clip. If the retainer is a bolt or a nut, hold the clutch and hub with the appropriate tool, and install the bolt or nut. Torque to manufacturer's specifications.

If the compressor clutch compo-

Related Vehicle Systems Diagnosis And Repair

nents have been replaced with the compressor off the vehicle, reinstall the compressor and connect the pressure lines and electrical connection. Next, evacuate and recharge the A/C system using the appropriate method and equipment, and check for leaks. Finally, check system performance.

CLUTCH CYCLING

Cycling the compressor clutch is a simple way to control evaporator pressure and hence, its temperature. Whenever pressure approaches the high limit, the controls simply switch off the clutch until pressure drops. The clutch is turned off and on automatically to prevent the evaporator from icing up. During operation, the clutch may cycle on and off several times each minute. As the change in heat load on the evaporator affects system pressures, the compressor cycling rate automatically changes to achieve the desired temperature. However, if the clutch cycles rapidly, it may be a sign of low refrigerant charge.

It is important to visually inspect the wiring and connectors to the various cycling and protection devices to make sure they are intact. Check for loose or broken wire connections and improperly formed or damaged terminals. All connector terminals in the circuit should be carefully inspected to determine the proper contact tension. Use a mating terminal to test contact tension. Ensure that all grounds are clean and making good contact.

The A/C electrical circuit must be opened or closed on demand from the system, or by the driver. Current will flow only in a closed circuit. In the case of the A/C compressor, the system must be performing at its optimum in order for the circuit to close, and the compressor clutch to engage. So, proper operation of all compressor clutch control switches is crucial to maintain system performance levels.

CLUTCH RELAY

The relay is composed of a coil and a set of contacts. When current is passed through the coil, a magnetic field is formed, and this field causes the contacts to move together, completing the circuit. Most relays are normally open, preventing current from passing through.

The operation of the A/C clutch relay is directly affected by the A/C switch input circuit. When the switch is turned on, high pressure, low pressure and temperature switches sense the correct conditions, and the relay opens to complete the circuit to the compressor clutch. However, any changes in pressure or temperature sensed by the control switches that would indicate an out-of-range condition will shut off current to the relay, and disengage the compressor clutch.

THERMOSTATIC SWITCH

To cycle the compressor, most systems use a thermostatic switch. It has a capillary tube attached to the evaporator outlet or inserted between the evaporator core fins to sense the temperature. This capillary is attached to a switch, which opens and closes as necessary to cycle the compressor. Most thermostatic switches are factory-set and not adjustable. If the switch is defective, the compressor clutch will cycle on and off quickly.

The more modern controls use a thermistor, which reacts faster than a mechanical thermostat to sense temperature changes. This keeps the temperature constant, as opposed to the temperature swings that are typical of mechanical thermostats. Additionally, thermistors do not need the constant airflow necessary to operate mechanical thermostats.

Although some expansion tube systems also use a thermostatic switch to control compressor clutch cycling, others use a pressure cycling switch. It senses the low side pressure (which is directly proportionate to temperature) near the evaporator outlet. Usually the pressure cycling switch is found on the accumulator, and is often mounted in a Schrader fitting so it can be replaced without the loss of refrigerant. When system pressure is low, the switch opens; when it is high the switch closes. The more heat the refrigerant picks up in the evaporator core, the higher the pressure becomes.

On expansion valve systems, the compressor is switched on at around 25 psi and off at about 10 psi. Expansion tube systems usually switch on at around 45 psi and turn off at 25 psi. Since system pressure is quite low during cold weather, the pressure cycling switch keeps the compressor from running when it isn't needed. It also protects the compressor from damage should the refrigerant charge escape.

BLOWER MOTOR

If the blower doesn't work, check the fuse or breaker, and check for voltage at the connector at the resistor block. If the blower doesn't work on high speed, the problem could be the high-speed relay or a fuse. Don't overlook the switch on the dashboard or the ground for the blower motor. If the blower is too slow at all speeds, perform a current draw test to see if the windings or brushes are bad. Noises from the blower could point to a bad bearing or debris in the fan.

Note that blown fuses or breakers most often indicate a short circuit in the wiring. However, a short can sometimes occur in the blower motor itself. It is obvious that for the motor to work, two things are necessary, power (voltage) to the motor, and continuity to ground. So, the first thing to check for is voltage available at the motor. While a 12-volt test light will indicate whether voltage is present, a DMM will tell you just how much voltage is present.

Related Vehicle Systems Diagnosis And Repair

To test for proper voltage, place the panel selector levers in the manufacturer's recommended positions and insert the probes of a DMM into the back of the connector at the blower motor. Check the measured voltage against manufacturer's specifications.

To test for blower motor current draw, disconnect the blower motor wire connector and connect a DMM (in the AMPS position) between the positive terminal on the motor and the corresponding terminal of the wire connector. Connect a jumper wire between the ground terminal on the motor and the corresponding terminal of the wire harness connector.

Place the panel selector levers in the manufacturer's recommended positions and start the engine. Operate the blower at all speeds, recording the current draw for each speed. Compare against manufacturer's specifications.

The blower motor is located underneath the dash, usually in the heater box with the heater core and the evaporator. If warm air is called for, the heater control valve is opened via the dash switch and hot coolant is directed through the heater core. Because the blower is located at the core, when it is activated, it will force warm air into the cab.

The same is true for cold air, except that coolant flow is shut off by the heater control valve, and when the air conditioner is activated, the blower forces cold air into the cab using the evaporator core as its air-cooling instrument.

If the blower works on one speed only, you know that the blower motor is functioning. The trouble then would have to be in the switch or resistor. For slower speeds, current is routed through one or more resistors in a resistor block, which is often found in the plenum where airflow can keep the resistor coils cool. Failure to work on one or more blower speeds means that a portion of the resistor assembly is probably burned out or the high-speed relay is defective. Also keep in mind that with today's modern systems, scan tools similar to those used to diagnose drivability problems can be used to diagnose HVAC electronic controls.

ELECTRIC COOLING FAN

Besides not needing a drive belt, electric fans conserve energy since they run only when needed. When the engine warms up, the electric fan should run. It may cycle on and off as the coolant warms and cools. The fan should also run whenever the A/C switch is activated. Some trucks have two fans with one dedicated to the A/C system that may not run for engine cooling alone.

If the fan doesn't run, check for power at its connector using a 12-volt test light. If there is power, suspect a faulty fan motor. If there is no power, the problem may be a blown fuse, the fan's temperature switch (often, but not always located in the radiator tank), the fan relay, the engine-control temperature sensor, the computer controls or the wiring. In most cases, the fan motor can be replaced by removing the entire assembly, and then removing the fan from its motor. Use caution not to damage the radiator fins or core tubes when removing the fan.

HIGH-PRESSURE CUTOUT SWITCH

When certain malfunctions occur, high-side pressures could exceed the safe operating limits of the compressor, hoses, or other components. To prevent this from happening, many

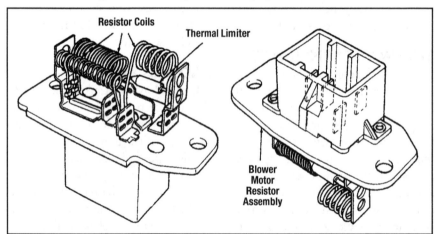

Typical blower motor resistor.

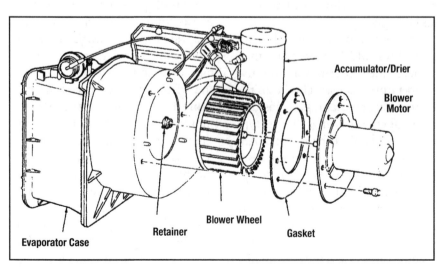

Typical blower motor and related components.

Related Vehicle Systems Diagnosis And Repair

systems are equipped with high-pressure cutout switches. These switches open the clutch circuit in the event that pressures become excessive. This function shuts down the compressor and stops the pressure from climbing higher. This serves two purposes: it protects the compressor from damage, and prevents venting of refrigerant through the pressure relief device (if equipped). Once repairs are made, the switch will allow normal clutch engagement. Note that many R12 systems and virtually all R134a systems are equipped with high-pressure cutout switches.

A quick way to check the high-pressure cutout switch operation is to connect the manifold gauge assembly, start the engine and engage the A/C system. To create a high pressure situation, restrict airflow through the condenser. The compressor should disengage once the pressure reaches the threshold of the switch calibration.

To replace the switch, disconnect the negative battery cable and the electrical connector to the switch. Remove the switch from the valve and discard the O-ring. Install the replacement switch with a new O-ring, connect the electrical connector and the negative battery cable. Finally, check system performance.

LOW-PRESSURE CUTOUT SWITCH

Some vehicles are equipped with low-pressure cut-off switches. The purpose of this switch is also compressor protection. The compressor clutch circuit is opened if the pressure in the system drops too low. This would be an indication that the system has lost some or all of its refrigerant charge. Since the lubricating oil is carried by the refrigerant, a loss could cause damage to the compressor if it were allowed to operate without sufficient lubrication.

To check the low-pressure cutout

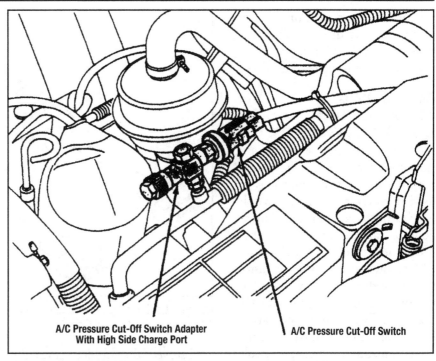

Some high pressure cutout switches are located at the high side service port of the A/C system.

switch, disconnect the electrical connector and connect a jumper wire across the terminals. Start the engine and engage the A/C system. If the compressor engages after a brief period, suspect a defective low-pressure cutout switch. If the compressor does not engage, the wiring, fuse or ambient temperature switch may be defective. If the clutch engages, connect a manifold gauge set, read the compressor discharge pressure and compare with manufacturer's specifications. At a specified pressure and ambient temperature, the switch should engage the compressor.

Unless the system has been completely discharged due to a leak, recover the refrigerant using the appropriate method and equipment before servicing the switch. Remove the switch and its O-ring from its mounting. Install the replacement switch with a new O-ring. Next, evacuate and recharge the A/C system and check for leaks. Finally, check system performance.

BINARY AND TRINARY SWITCHES

Trucks equipped with a Red Dot A/C system may have either a Binary or Trinary switch to protect the compressor. Both types automatically reset when system pressures return to normal. The Binary switch protects against low pressure and high pressure problems by interrupting current flow to the compressor clutch. It is located in the high-pressure (liquid) side of the system between the condenser and the expansion valve or expansion tube.

The Binary switch protects the system from two conditions. If the pressure drops to between 3-15 psi, the Binary switch opens. When the pressure returns to 40 psi, it closes again. Likewise, if pressure builds up to over 270-330 psi, the Binary switch opens and then closes when the pressure drops back down to between 80-120 psi.

In addition to high- and low-pressure situations, the Trinary switch has a mid-range function. Also located in the high-pressure (liquid)

Training for Certification

Related Vehicle Systems Diagnosis And Repair

side of the A/C circuit (most often on the receiver-drier), it also controls the engine cooling fan or radiator shutters to increase air flow.

AUTOMATIC TEMPERATURE CONTROL (ATC)

In ATC systems, the electric and vacuum controls are combined. For example, an electric motor may be used to operate a vacuum switch, which sends vacuum to the various air doors or water valve control switches.

On some trucks, especially those with automatic temperature control, the mode doors are moved by DC motors that push or pull levers as necessary. Total failure indicates a blown fuse. But if individual components malfunction, check for voltage to the motor and check the motor itself.

The most common cause of electrical failure is a blown fuse or circuit breaker. Most systems have a power fuse in the fuse block, but occasionally there is an additional in-line fuse in the circuit to the blower relay, for high speed only.

There are several important things to remember when you work on automatic systems. Always start by checking the less complicated items first, just as if the truck had a manual A/C system. Inspect the air or vacuum supply in addition to the lines and hoses. It is possible that the problem could be caused by leaks in lines, fittings and unions.

Start by doing a system performance check. Then, use a heat gun or hair dryer to warm the thermostat or the temperature sensor (thermistor). The system should respond with cooler air out of the dash outlets. Next, chill the airflow to the sensor to produce the opposite effect. Note the reaction or lack of it.

If the system reacts to a change to one input, but not to the other, the problem is most likely confined to the sensor or its circuit. But if no reaction

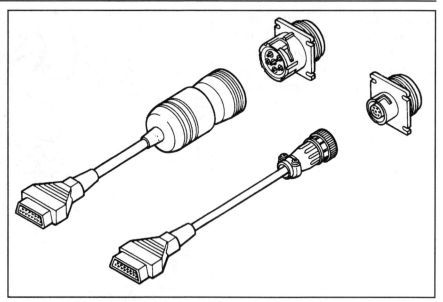

Diagnostic link connectors used with Detroit Series 60 diesel engines. *(Courtesy: Detroit Diesel Corp.)*

is observed, the problem is usually with the controller or its outputs.

ATC ELECTRICAL DIAGNOSTICS

The proper function of the ATC depends upon the electrical inputs of a number of sensors. The programming that enables the ECM to provide control of the system naturally tells the engine computer how to interpret these signals. To help the technician find trouble, the computer is instructed to know the difference between a reasonable sensor input and one that indicates the sensor is not functioning properly.

Should the system begin to operate erratically, the ECM will record that fact and remember a fault code that will tell the technician what has happened. The goal of this system is not only to lead the technician in the right direction, but also to retain information about a fault that might be intermittent and may not be evident when the truck is brought in for service.

First of all, it is important to check these basics:
- Fuses, fusible links and wiring
- Coolant level
- Heater core and water valve operation
- Refrigerant charge and compressor operation
- Tension of compressor drive belt
- Tightness of vacuum line connections
- Radiator airflow and coolant flow through the thermostat
- Radiator fan operation.

If the control panel has a digital display, the temperature indication on the display would be replaced by the failure code number when in the diagnostic mode. Start the engine and let it warm up to operating temperature. Following the manufacturer's instructions, activate the digital display to read the diagnostic codes. Record all codes displayed during the test. If error codes appear during the test, follow the diagnostic procedures outlined by the manufacturer.

If the control panel does not have a digital display, connect a suitable scan tool to the diagnostic data link and read active or stored diagnostic codes. Compare these codes with the manufacturer's trouble code list to pinpoint the problem.

Related Vehicle Systems Diagnosis And Repair

IN-CAB TEMPERATURE SENSOR

The automatic and semi-automatic air conditioning units use a sensor that monitors the temperature in the cab. The sensor is mounted underneath the dash and air is drawn over it by the blower airstream through an aspirator tube. Vacuum supplied to the sensor valve is modulated according to temperature.

Sensor temperature calibration is adjusted by the temperature setting at the system control panel via cable from the panel lever arm to the sensor lever. If the driver moves the control lever to a higher or lower control setting, the cable moves the lever on the sensor, which changes its vacuum control calibration.

To check the sensor, make sure there is appropriate vacuum and operate the temperature lever at the control panel. Check to see if the cable moves the lever on the sensor. Monitor the output vacuum of the sensor to see if it moves the mechanical arm connected to the blend door linkage.

The sensor is replaced by removing any dash components that may impede its removal, and then disconnecting the sensor tube from the assembly. Remove the sensor screws from the instrument panel bracket and remove the sensor.

AMBIENT TEMPERATURE SWITCH

The function of the ambient temperature switch is to inhibit compressor clutch operation in cold ambient temperatures. This sensor opens the electrical path to the compressor clutch when the temperature is below a specified range. This function mainly protects the compressor from poor or no lubrication, which could be the result of cold refrigerant oil.

The ambient temperature sensor is located outside the vehicle, often just behind the grille or in some other "up front" location.

To check the sensor, disconnect the connector and connect a jumper wire across the sensor terminals. Start the engine and activate the A/C to the manufacturer's recommended temperature. If the compressor clutch engages, suspect a defective ambient temperature sensor.

REFRIGERANT SOLENOID VALVE

Used in trucks with sleepers, the refrigerant solenoid valve regulates the amount of refrigerant entering the sleeper evaporator. Most solenoids are designed to fail in the closed position in order to keep the front air conditioning performing at maximum output. The electronically-controlled solenoid valve is controlled by the ECM and delivers the correct refrigerant flow based on changes in engine speed and load.

Insufficient cooling in the sleeper can be the result of solenoid valve failure. This can be due to burned out coil windings, improper or no current, dirt, corrosion or sludge in the valve piston, or evaporator icing due to the solenoid being stuck in the open position.

If the refrigerant solenoid valve is suspect, connect a suitable scan tool to the diagnostic data link and read active or stored diagnostic codes. Compare these codes with the manufacturer's trouble code list.

Unless the system has been completely discharged due to a leak, recover the refrigerant using the appropriate method and equipment before servicing the solenoid. Disconnect the refrigerant lines and remove the solenoid. Install the replacement solenoid with a new refrigerant line O-ring. Next, evacuate and recharge the A/C system and check for leaks.

Finally, check system performance.

ELECTRONIC CONTROL HEAD

The electronic control head incorporates a system of rotary dials and push buttons. This control head is mounted on the instrument panel and usually attached to an electronic control module. When the switches in the control head are activated, signals are sent to the A/C electronic control module, which in turn, operates the A/C system.

When the control panel experiences a malfunction, a trouble code is sent to the A/C electronic control module. Connect a suitable scan tool to the diagnostic data link and read active or stored diagnostic codes. Compare these codes with the manufacturer's trouble code list.

To replace the control head, disconnect the negative battery cable and remove all necessary instrument panel components to gain access to the control head. Carefully remove the control head from the instrument panel and disconnect all electrical leads. After installation, reconnect the negative battery cable and check for proper operation.

ELECTRONIC CONTROL MODULE

The electronic control module manages all of the A/C system's electronic functions. It electronically operates the A/C compressor and various door actuators. It also retains the operator's selected settings when the vehicle is not running and measures return inputs from the various sensors. After measuring all input information, the computer will complete the output circuits to provide signals for system regulation.

To replace the electronic control module, disconnect the negative battery cable and remove all necessary instrument panel components to gain access to the module. Remove the screws that fasten the control module to its mounting. Pull the unit out to expose the wires and

Related Vehicle Systems Diagnosis And Repair

unplug them. Remove the control module from the instrument panel. After installation, reconnect the negative battery cable and check for proper operation.

POTENTIOMETER

Some vehicles have a potentiometer located in the HVAC electronic control module that relays the position of the temperature control lever to the ECM. The ECM processes the information and air conditioning output is regulated accordingly.

To test the potentiometer, locate the air conditioning control module, and connect a DMM switched to the ohms position across the potentiometer wires at the end of the module connector. Check the resistance of the potentiometer while moving the temperature control lever. Check the readings against manufacturer's specifications.

If the readings are not within specifications, replace the potentiometer. Disconnect the negative battery cable and remove the HVAC control head from the instrument panel. Disconnect the potentiometer wiring and remove it from the HVAC control head.

SUN LOAD SENSOR (SOLAR SENSOR)

The sun load sensor is a photo diode usually mounted on the top of the dash. Varying amounts of sunlight striking it will modify its electrical return signal to the programmer. Bright sunlight will cause the programmer to adjust system output toward cooler air; less sunlight will cause the programmer to adjust system output toward warmer air. Some multi-zone climate control systems have more than one sun load sensor.

AUXILIARY POWER

Auxiliary power outlets are used in today's vehicles for a variety of functions. Of course, one outlet can be used as a cigarette lighter. However, additional outlets have been added to modern vehicles to power components such as personal computers, cell phones, etc. Equipped with a suitable adapter, the components can be plugged into the outlets and powered or charged accordingly.

Taking power supply a step further, DC to AC inverters are available to power household items such as televisions, refrigerators, microwave ovens, etc., converting the vehicle DC battery power to regular household AC.

Because of the relatively insecure connection of the power plug, some manufacturers are developing power outlets separate from the cigarette lighter style. These outlets will contain a standardized design that looks much like a standard 110-volt household wall plug.

Basically, there are two types of inverters: the standard inverter, which will enable the user to power household electrical devices, and the inverter/charger, which not only supplies power, but also enables truck battery charging via shore power.

Shore power is AC current supplied by an external source such as what you may see at many truck stops and truck terminals. When connected to shore power, all loads (DC and AC) can be powered by the inverter/charger in addition to truck battery charging capabilities. Note that a standard inverter can also be connected to shore power. However, it will not supply the battery charging capabilities of the inverter/charger.

Most inverters are internally protected from extreme voltage and temperature conditions.

If it is determined that one or more of these conditions exists for a specified amount of time, the inverter will shut itself down. Usually, the cause of inverter shutdown can be attributed to excessive loads applied to the unit. Make sure you are aware of these loads and always allow the manufacturer's recommended period of time before restarting.

If there is no or low AC voltage output from the inverter, check the battery(s), fuses or circuit breakers, and inspect for loose cable connections. If DC voltage exists at the inverter input, but no AC voltage exists at the outlet(s), check the wiring and connections from the inverter to the outlet.

If there is AC voltage at the back of the outlet, but no voltage from the outlet socket, suspect a defective outlet. If DC voltage exists at the inverter input and there is no AC voltage coming from the inverter, suspect a problem with the inverter itself.

With the inverter connected to AC shore power, check for AC voltage at the inverter input and at the outlet(s). If no AC voltage exists at the inverter input, check the wiring harness and connections between the shore power supply

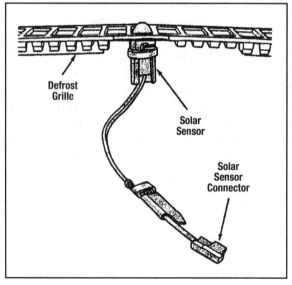

The sun (or solar) sensor is mounted on top of the instrument panel. It senses the intensity of sunlight and adjusts the ATC to meet the demand.

and the inverter.

Trucks can also be equipped with a low-voltage-disconnect (LVD). This component monitors battery voltage and disconnect the load when voltage is below normal. This helps to prevent over-discharge of the battery by shutting down accessories before battery failure.

The LVD is installed in line between the battery and the load, and monitors voltage. If voltage falls below specifications, the load is automatically disconnected, saving the batteries from complete discharge. When battery charging is restored, the load is automatically reconnected.

POWER WINDOWS

Power window motors are usually of the permanent magnet type. Reversing the direction of the current through the terminals of the motor reverses the motor's direction.

A power window circuit generally consists of window regulator motors and individual control switches at each door. The circuit also has a master switch by which all windows can be operated. Most systems are protected by a fuse or circuit breaker and receive power only when the ignition switch is in the ON position.

Typically, each motor is grounded through the switch. Both terminals of each window motor are connected to opposite and adjacent sides of the switch. Pushing the switch up will cause the motor to close the window. Pushing the switch down will cause it to open the window. The switch reverses current through the motor's terminals.

If all the windows fail to operate first check the circuit breaker or fuse, fusible link and master switch. Besides the wiring and its connectors, these components are the only ones that could affect the entire circuit. To check a circuit breaker, check for voltage on both sides of the breaker or fuse with the ignition on. If voltage is present on one side only, the breaker is defective or the fuse is blown.

To check the power window motor, remove the door panel and thoroughly check for any flaws that would prevent the motor and regulator assembly from moving or operating properly. Check for voltage at the motor with the switch depressed. If the proper voltage (12 volts) is present, and the motor still doesn't operate, replace the motor. If low or no voltage is present, causing the window to be inoperative or work slowly, check the wiring, connections and switches in the circuit for shorts.

To test the master switch, remove the switch from the door and check for voltage at the battery feed wire. If no voltage is present, check the wiring and connections between the fuse or circuit breaker and the switch connector and repair as necessary. If voltage is present, check for voltage across the switch from the battery feed wire to the switch's ground terminal. If voltage is present, the switch is OK. If no voltage is present, connect a voltmeter to the ground terminal and a good chassis ground. If voltage is present, repair the ground circuit. Often loose wires or connectors will cause the windows to work intermittently.

Check the individual switch as follows: Test the down position of the switch by jumping from the positive lead to the down terminal of the switch. Connect another jumper from the ground terminal of the switch to the up terminal. If the motor works, power is getting through. Put the switch back on the connector, and operate the switch. If the motor will not work, replace the switch.

REPLACEMENT

Window regulators are available in several different styles, including gear-and-sector, scissors lift or cable operated. To replace the regulator, remove the inside door panel and related components. Support the door glass in the full-up position. Disconnect the power connector at the motor.

NOTE: Window regulators can be riveted to the inside of the door panel. If this is the case, use a drill to remove the rivets. Use care not to enlarge the sheet metal holes in the door panel.

Remove the rivets or screws that hold the regulator to the door panel. Slide the regulator rearward while removing the regulator arm(s), gears, or cable from the glass bracket. Slide the regulator from the door assembly.

Slide the window regulator into the door assembly. Before installing

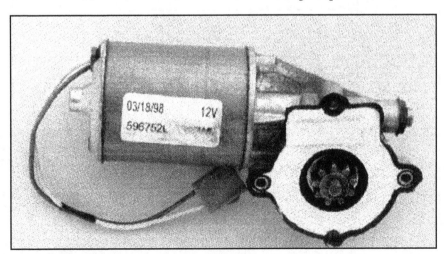

Typical window regulator motor.   *(Courtesy: ArvinMeritor Corp.)*

Related Vehicle Systems Diagnosis And Repair

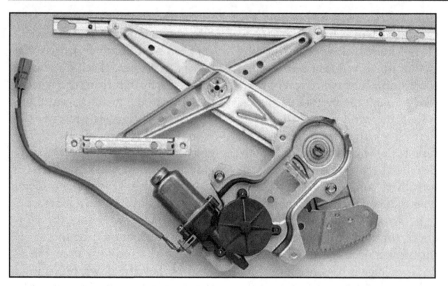

Typical scissors lift window regulator. *(Courtesy: ArvinMeritor Corporation)*

the rivets or screws, install the regulator arm(s), gears, or cable onto the glass bracket. Install new rivets or screws to hold the regulator in the door panel. Reconnect the wire connector and check operation and adjustment. After the regulator is working properly, install the door panel and related components.

Depending on the vehicle, the regulator motor can be replaced with the window regulator in or out of the vehicle. To replace the regulator motor, disconnect the negative battery cable and remove the door panel along with any related components. Disconnect the wire connector at the motor. Remove the window regulator if necessary. Remove the motor mounting bolts and the motor from the window regulator.

Install the replacement motor onto the window regulator and install the mounting bolts. If removed, install the window regulator. Reconnect the wire connector and check for proper operation. If the motor is working properly, install the door panel and related components.

POWER DOOR LOCKS

Power to the door lock circuit is usually provided via a circuit breaker or fuse, which is in turn, powered directly by the battery. The door lock function doesn't rely on the ignition switch for its power.

When the switch is pressed to the lock position, current flows to the door lock motor. This energizes the motor, causing a plunger to move inward. The plunger is connected to the standard lock linkage. So, when the plunger travels inward the door locks, and when it moves outward, the door unlocks.

When the door lock switch is moved to the unlock position, current flows to the door lock motor in the opposite direction. Many newer vehicles use relays to control the

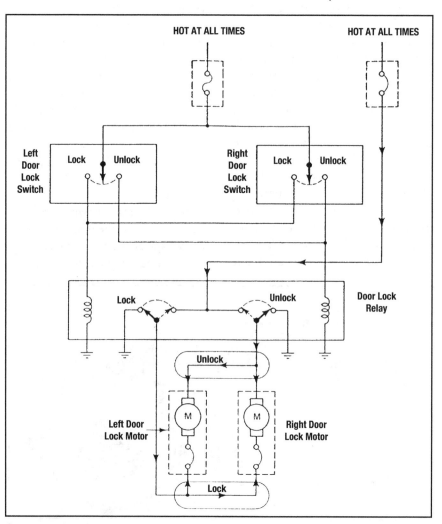

Common door lock system.

60   T6 - Electrical/Electronic Systems

Related Vehicle Systems Diagnosis And Repair

locks so the switches do not bear the load-carrying burden, but only provide current to the relay.

NOTE: Always make sure the door lock motor is mounted properly and the linkage is not bent or binding before condemning the door lock motor or switch. This can cause poor or intermittent operation of the door locks.

Test the switch by checking for power at the feed circuit of the switch. If there is no power, check the fuse, circuit breaker, wiring and connectors upstream from the switch. If there is power, install a jumper wire from the positive lead to the lock terminal of the switch. Connect another jumper from the ground terminal of the switch to the unlock terminal. If the door lock motor works, power is getting through. Put the switch back on the connector, and operate the switch. If the door lock motor will not work, replace the switch.

To check the door lock motor, remove the door panel and check for 12 volts at the feed circuit when the switch is activated. If there is no power, check the wiring and connections from the switch to the motor. If there is power, the door lock motor should work. If the motor doesn't work, replace it.

To remove the motor, disconnect the actuator motor link from the door latch. Remove the screw or rivet that attaches the actuator motor to the door and disconnect the wiring at the connector. Then, remove the motor. To install, connect the wire connector and install the motor in the door using a new rivet or screw. Connect the motor link to the door latch. Use care not to twist the actuator boot upon installation.

CRUISE CONTROL

The cruise or speed control system allows the driver to travel at a constant speed without maintaining foot pressure on the throttle pedal.

If the speed control is inoperative, start with a visual inspection of the components that make up the system. Check for exposed, broken, disconnected or damaged wiring. Check the throttle actuator and throttle linkage to make sure it is operating properly. Correct all problems uncovered by the visual inspection before proceeding with further system tests.

To check the control switches, on/off circuits, and set/accelerate/coast/resume circuits, first check the fuse. If the fuse is OK, disconnect the wire connector at the amplifier assembly. The amplifier's function is to keep a steady throttle speed as desired by the driver. Check for battery voltage and resistance at the connector pins specified by the particular manufacturer. If resistance values are above specifications, suspect the switch assemblies or a problem with the wiring or connectors in the circuit.

To test the speed sensor, raise and safely support the drive wheels. Disconnect the wire connector located on the transmission housing. Connect an ohmmeter between the terminals of the speed sensor and compare the readings with manufacturer's specifications.

Next, place the vehicle in gear and allow the wheels to rotate. The ohmmeter should fluctuate. If it does not, or the reading is not within specifications, replace the sensor. Apply the brakes, take the vehicle out of gear, reconnect the wire connector and lower the vehicle.

The amplifier senses brake light voltage when the driver depresses the brake pedal. This in turn disengages the cruise control. The amplifier also checks for resistance to ground through the brake light bulbs. If the ground is not detected, operation is interrupted because it detects that the wire to the brake light switch may be broken. This means that on some models, if both brake lights are burned out, the cruise control won't work.

To check the brake light switch on vehicles with air brakes, check for voltage at the electrical connection. If there is no voltage, check the fuse and wiring. If voltage is present, install an air gauge in the service line and gradually apply the brakes. The stoplights should illuminate at 6 psi or less. Check for air leaks at the switch. No air leaks are permissible.

If the vehicle is equipped with hydraulic brakes, check for voltage at the switch. If there is no voltage, check the fuse and wiring. If voltage is present, activate the switch and check for voltage on the opposite side of the switch. If voltage is not present, replace the switch assembly. If voltage is present, check the wiring, bulbs and connections in the stoplight circuit downstream of the stoplight switch and repair as necessary.

Manual transmission models employ a clutch switch that opens and disengages the cruise control circuit when the clutch pedal is depressed. When the pedal is released, the system will stay disengaged.

The clutch switch is wired in with the brake light switch so that it breaks the circuit to the brake light bulbs. Due to the safety feature mentioned with the brake lights, the systems disengage.

To check the clutch switch, remove the electrical connector and, using an ohmmeter, check resistance at the switch against manufacturer's specifications. If values are within specification, the switch is OK. If resistance values are not within specification, replace the clutch switch.

ELECTRIC TRANSFER (LIFT) PUMP

Some trucks have electric transfer pumps, or lift pumps, that bring fuel from the fuel tank to the injection pump. The electric transfer pump is

Related Vehicle Systems Diagnosis And Repair

mounted as a separate unit. Its purpose is to move the fuel from the storage tank, through a strainer and fuel filter to the rest of the system at low pressure. There are several types of pumps in use depending on manufacturer preference and engine application. However, they operate mostly in the same manner. Once activated, the pump creates a vacuum that pulls fuel at low pressure from the tank to the injection pump.

Failure symptoms include hunting idle, excessive white smoke, stumbling on acceleration, no start, or slow start conditions. The lift pump may even fail to the point that it will set a trouble code.

To check lift pump operation, disable the disconnect the line between the lift pump and the injection pump. Have an assistant crank the engine. If you hear the pump working and observe fuel flow, it is operating properly. If you do not hear the pump working or there is no fuel flow, suspect either a problem in the lift pump circuit or a defective lift pump.

Notes

Prepare yourself for ASE testing with these questions on MEDIUM/HEAVY ELECTRICAL/ELECTRONIC SYSTEMS

NOTE: The following questions are written in the ASE style. They are similar to the kinds of questions that you will see on the ASE test. However, none of these questions will actually appear on the test.

1. A technician needs to check for voltage in a non-solid state electrical circuit. Technician A says a 12-volt test light can be used by attaching one lead to a known good voltage source, then probing various points along the circuit. Technician B says one lead of the 12-volt test light should be grounded, and the other used to probe various points along the circuit. Who is right?
   A. Technician A only
   B. Technician B only
   C. Both A and B
   D. Neither A or B

2. Technician A says an ohmmeter can be used instead of a self-powered test light when checking continuity. Technician B says a multimeter set to ohms can be used to back-probe for voltage. Who is right?
   A. Technician A only
   B. Technician B only
   C. Both A and B
   D. Neither A or B

Questions 3 through 8 are based on the following schematic:

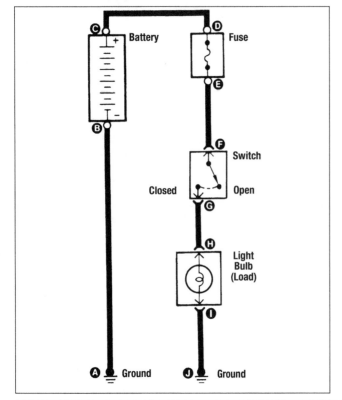

3. In the previous circuit, the light bulb will not light. The fuse is good, and there is voltage at point F. With the switch closed, there is no voltage at point G. What is the likely cause?
   A. There is a bad ground at point J.
   B. The battery terminals are loose.
   C. The bulb is bad.
   D. The switch or its connection is bad.

4. In order to bench test the switch in this circuit, a technician would use:
   A. a test light
   B. a voltmeter
   C. a self-powered test light
   D. an ammeter

5. With the switch in the circuit closed, there is voltage at point H, but the light still doesn't work. Technician A says it could be a bad bulb. Technician B says it could be a bad ground. Who is right?
   A. Technician A only
   B. Technician B only
   C. Both A and B
   D. Neither A or B

6. If you concluded that the bulb in this circuit was not grounded, how could you check for a break in the ground wire?
   A. attach a 12-volt test light or voltmeter to points G and H
   B. attach a self-powered test light or ohmmeter to points G and H
   C. attach a 12-volt test light or voltmeter to points I and J
   D. attach a self-powered test light or ohmmeter to points I and J

7. Same circuit, new symptoms: the light doesn't work and the fuse is blown. You replace the fuse, but as soon as you attempt to operate the circuit, the new fuse blows. What could be the problem?
   A. There is a short to ground.
   B. The fuse is too low an amperage rating.
   C. both A and B
   D. neither A or B

64   T6 - Electrical/Electronic Systems

Prepare yourself for ASE testing with these questions on MEDIUM/HEAVY ELECTRICAL/ELECTRONIC SYSTEMS

8. In the previous example, the fault is a short to ground. Technician A says it must be between points G and H. Technician B says it could be between points E and H. Who is right?
   A. Technician A only
   B. Technician B only
   C. Both A and B
   D. Neither A or B

9. Technician A says the two most common types of circuit breakers are thermal and non-conductive. Technician B says all circuit breakers can be manually reset. Who is right?
   A. Technician A
   B. Technician B
   C. Both A and B
   D. Neither A or B

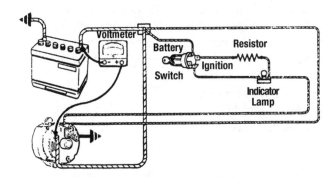

10. In the charging system shown above, the meter reading will show:
    A. charging output voltage
    B. indicator light operating voltage
    C. charging circuit voltage drop
    D. ignition switch voltage drop

11. Fiber optics transmit light along great distances by using which of the following?
    A. glass
    B. semi-insulated wire
    C. light emitting diodes
    D. metallic conductors

12. A high rate discharge test (battery capacity test) is being performed on a 12-volt battery. Technician A says that a good battery should have a voltage reading below 7 volts while under load. Technician B says that the battery should be discharged (loaded) at two times its ampere hour rating. Who is right?
    A. Technician A only
    B. Technician B only
    C. Both A and B
    D. Neither A or B

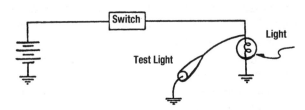

13. The light in the circuit shown above glows dimly. A technician connects a 12-volt test light as shown. The test light burns at normal brightness. Technician A says that a bad ground at the light could be the cause. Technician B says that high resistance in the circuit from the battery to the light could be the cause. Who is right?
    A. Technician A only
    B. Technician B only
    C. Both A and B
    D. Neither A or B

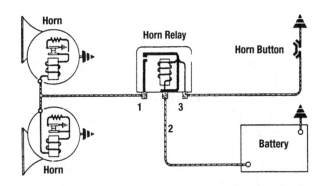

14. The horns in the circuit shown above only blow when a jumper wire is connected between terminals #1 and #2 of the horn relay. Technician A says that a bad horn relay could be the cause. Technician B says that a ground in the circuit between the horn relay and the horn button could be the cause. Who is right?
    A. Technician A only
    B. Technician B only
    C. Both A and B
    D. Neither A or B

Training for Certification

Prepare yourself for ASE testing with these questions on MEDIUM/HEAVY ELECTRICAL/ELECTRONIC SYSTEMS

15. Technician A says a noisy alternator could be caused by a bad diode. Technician B says a noisy alternator could be caused by a worn bearing. Who is right?
    A. Technician A only
    B. Technician B only
    C. Both A and B
    D. Neither A or B

16. On a vehicle with a 12-volt system, a circuit feeds a pair of 50-watt auxiliary lights. Technician A says a 5-amp fuse is OK to use in the circuit. Technician B says to find the proper amp fuse, you must first use a mathematical equation. Who is right?
    A. Technician A only
    B. Technician B only
    C. Both A and B
    D. Neither A or B

17. A technician finds that a truck's four batteries have all frozen solid. The outside air temperature is –10°F. Technician A says the problem is the truck was parked outside at too low a temperature. Technician B says the truck's batteries were allowed to discharge too deeply. Who is right?
    A. Technician A only
    B. Technician B only
    C. Both A and B
    D. Neither A or B

18. A truck has experienced a rapid failure of one of its four batteries. The failed battery is much newer than the other three. The remaining batteries are still usable, but accept a charge only very slowly. Technician A says all four batteries must be replaced to prevent a recurrence of the problem. Technician B says the one bad battery experienced a random failure, and should simply be replaced. Who is right?
    A. Technician A only
    B. Technician B only
    C. Both A and B
    D. Neither A or B

19. The alternator on a vehicle has failed prematurely. Basic checks of vehicle wiring and batteries have revealed no problems, but the driver has left the lights on overnight several times. Each time, the vehicle was jump-started and sent back out. Technician A says the alternator was probably defective and replacing it should solve the problem. Technician B says the problem is that the vehicle's batteries should have been slow-charged before sending the truck back out on the road. Who is right?
    A. Technician A only
    B. Technician B only
    C. Both A and B
    D. Neither A or B

20. An over-the-road truck that has experienced excellent electrical system performance is switched to city delivery service. Idling restrictions require that the truck be shut off and restarted at every stop. Now, the vehicle has a chronic problem with undercharged batteries and failure to start. Technician A says the truck needs a larger alternator and batteries. Technician B says the voltage regulator should be rated higher to provide a faster charging rate. Who is right?
    A. Technician A only
    B. Technician B only
    C. Both A and B
    D. Neither A or B

21. Some fiber optics use which of the following to change light signals to electrical signals.
    A. igniters
    B. reluctors
    C. transducers
    D. pulse generators

22. Daytime running lights are usually illuminated at which of the following intensity?
    A. 50% or less of normal intensity
    B. 70% or less of normal intensity
    C. 30% or less of normal intensity
    D. 100% of normal inteslty

Prepare yourself for ASE testing with these questions on MEDIUM/HEAVY ELECTRICAL/ELECTRONIC SYSTEMS

23. A truck has experienced a charging problem. A careful technician has found loose mounting bolts on the alternator and tightened them. The truck now performs well. Technician A says the problem might have been a slipping belt. Technician B says the problem might have been poor grounding of the alternator. Who is right?
    A. Technician A only
    B. Technician B only
    C. Both A and B
    D. Neither A or B

24. A diesel truck with a late model engine is experiencing occasional starting problems. A check of the alternator rating vs. total accessory load has determined that the alternator rating is sufficient. Technician A says there must be a charging system malfunction. Technician B says the problem might be solved by replacing the present alternator with a design that has the same peak rating, but produces it at a lower minimum rpm. Who is right?
    A. Technician A only
    B. Technician B only
    C. Both A and B
    D. Neither A or B

25. An oil pressure warning light fails to illuminate, even when the engine is shut down. All of the following are possible causes of the problem EXCEPT:
    A. defective sending unit
    B. grounded wire from the light to the sending unit
    C. high-resistance connection between the sending unit and the wiring coming from the warning light
    D. burned-out warning light bulb

26. The following are all effective ways to determine that a battery is at full charge EXCEPT:
    A. consistently trouble-free starting
    B. temperature-corrected specific gravity of 1.260-1.270 in each cell
    C. an open post voltage of 12.66 volts with the surface charge removed
    D. a stable, low rate of charge from a constant-voltage type charger

27. The following are all possible causes of a poor starter ground EXCEPT:
    A. loose mounting bolts
    B. missing starter ground strap
    C. missing engine-to-frame ground strap
    D. corroded cab mounts

28. All of the following are basic starter solenoid voltage checks EXCEPT:
    A. voltage between S terminal and ground
    B. voltage between G connector and ground
    C. voltage drop between B terminal and motor terminal
    D. voltage between S terminal and G terminal

29. All of the following are major advantages of LED lighting over incandescent lighting EXCEPT:
    A. they are visibly brighter
    B. they are more expensive
    C. they consume less power
    D. they cast more light outward

30. The driver of a vehicle is complaining that the horn is not working. Technician A says to disarm the Supplemental Restraint System (SRS) before servicing the horn button. Technician B says to examine the horn to see if it can be adjusted before replacing it. Who is right?
    A. Technician A only
    B. Technician B only
    C. Both A and B
    D. Neither A or B

31. An air conditioning check has uncovered a discharge in the system and compressor damage. Technician A says that after the repairs are made, to check the low-pressure cutoff switch. Technician B says lubricating oil is carried by the refrigerant through the system. Who is right?
    A. Technician A only
    B. Technician B only
    C. Both A and B
    D. Neither A or B

Prepare yourself for ASE testing with these questions on MEDIUM/HEAVY ELECTRICAL/ELECTRONIC SYSTEMS

32. Technician A says when soldering, it is best to remove the component from the vehicle and place it on a metal surface. Technician B says once a soldering tip no longer transfers heat quickly, it should be replaced. Who is right?
   A. Technician A
   B. Technician B
   C. Both A and B
   D. Neither A or B

33. A starter system is being checked and the starter motor has been found to be overheated. Technician A says the starter was overheated due to excessive cranking. Technician B says if a starter gets too hot while cranking, it should be cooled using compressed air. Who is right?
   A. Technician A only
   B. Technician B only
   C. Both A and B
   D. Neither A or B

34. The best tool to use when checking a key-off battery drain is:
   A. analog multimeter
   B. 12-volt test light
   C. DMM with resistor pack
   D. oscilloscope

35. A windshield washer system is being checked. Fluid is spraying from the nozzle on the passenger side, but not on the driver's side. Of the following possibilities, which could be the cause?
   A. blown fuse
   B. no voltage at the pump
   C. low fluid level
   D. kinked or blocked hose

36. Technician A says that if a wire is getting too hot, it's a sign of higher-than-normal current flowing through the wire. Technician B says the wire would heat up if some of the individual strands were broken inside the wire insulation. Who is right?
   A. Technician A only
   B. Technician B only
   C. Both A and B
   D. Neither A or B

37. Technician A says if one or two speeds do not work on a blower motor, the problem could be a defective capacitor. Technician B says a capacitor is a device for controlling the direction of electron flow. Who is right?
   A. Technician A only
   B. Technician B only
   C. Both A and B
   D. Neither A or B

38. An over-the-road truck equipped with sleeper air conditioning is experiencing warm air from the sleeper ducts only. Of the following, which could be the cause?
   A. inoperative solenoid valve
   B. defective ambient temperature sensor
   C. defective solar sensor
   D. low refrigerant

39. When testing computer-controlled systems, a Digital Multimeter (DMM) should be used with an input impedance of at least:
   A. 10k ohms
   B. 100k ohms
   C. 1 megohm
   D. 10 megohms

40. Technician A says a short circuit to ground will decrease resistance. Technician B says a short circuit will increase current flow. Who is right?
   A. Technician A only
   B. Technician B only
   C. Both A and B
   D. Neither A or B

41. What is the purpose of a high-pressure cutoff switch in an air conditioning system?
   A. interrupts compressor voltage in the event of high system pressures
   B. interrupts compressor voltage in the event of low accumulator pressures
   C. interrupts compressor voltage and increases cooling fan speed
   D. relieves pressure buildup due to a signal from ambient temperature sensor

Prepare yourself for ASE testing with these questions on MEDIUM/HEAVY ELECTRICAL/ELECTRONIC SYSTEMS

42. Which setting on a digital multimeter is used to check resistance?
    A. millivolt
    B. milliamp
    C. ohms
    D. voltage

43. Technician A says that ECM codes can be cleared on a truck using a diagnostic scan tool. Technician B says that codes can be cleared on some older trucks by disconnecting the power source for a brief period of time. Who is right?
    A. Technician A only
    B. Technician B only
    C. Both A and B
    D. Neither A or B

44. By adjusting a percent-of-charge switch, some high-rate discharge (load) testers will test a battery with a charge as low as.
    A. 10%
    B. 15%
    C. 20%
    D. 25%

45. A driver of a combination vehicle says that when a trailer is connected to the tractor, the trailer turn signals do not work. However, when the trailer is disconnected, the tractor turn signals work OK. Technician A says to check for power at the green and yellow wires of the light cord plug. Technician B says to check the fuse for the tractor turn signals. Who is right?
    A. Technician A only
    B. Technician B only
    C. Both A and B
    D. Neither A or B

46. Technician A says that the batteries on a tractor should be covered by a fixed part of the vehicle. Technician B says a removable cover must be used. Who is right?
    A. Technician A only
    B. Technician B only
    C. Both A and B
    D. Neither A or B

47. The alternator/voltage regulator is designed to keep voltage output on a 12-volt system at:
    A. 12.5-13.5 volts
    B. 13.0-14.0 volts
    C. 13.5-14.5 volts
    D. 14.5-15.5 volts

48. The clutch switch is designed to:
    A. open the cruise control circuit
    B. help with clutch shifting
    C. close the cruise control circuit
    D. none of the above

49. Voltage drop tests are used to locate:
    A. low resistance
    B. shorts
    C. opens
    D. high resistance

50. In a charging system, AC is converted to DC via the:
    A. voltage regulator
    B. brushes
    C. rectifying diodes
    D. stator

51. A truck that uses multiple AC sockets for different accessories comes in unable to receive power to one of the interior accessories. Technician A says to inspect the outlet socket for AC power. Technician B says to check for DC voltage at the inverter input. Who is right?
    A. Technician A only
    B. Technician B only
    C. Both A and B
    D. Neither A or B

52. A truck driver complains that his AC-powered refrigerator shuts off after a period of time when the vehicle is off. The vehicle is equipped with a Low-Voltage-Discharge (LVD) unit. What should the technician check first?
    A. the LVD unit
    B. for a short at the AC socket
    C. battery charge
    D. refrigerator

Training for Certification

Prepare yourself for ASE testing with these questions on MEDIUM/HEAVY ELECTRICAL/ELECTRONIC SYSTEMS

53. A truck driver complains that the dashboard gauges fluctuate in similar patterns while driving. Technician A says all dashboards use a voltage regulator. Technician B says the dashboard voltage regulator supplies a constant 5 volts to all the dash gauges. Who is right?
    A. Technician A only
    B. Technician B only
    C. Both A and B
    D. Neither A or B

54. LED bulbs can remain effective for up to:
    A. 200 hours
    B. 1000 hours
    C. 50,000 hours
    D. 100,000 hours

55. A remote sensing alternator is designed to:
    A. allow for operation of remote accessories
    B. recognize overcharging and adjust charging voltage
    C. monitor AC power from the inverter
    D. recognize actual vehicle load requirements

56. The current protocol used for truck data communication is:
    A. J-1157
    B. J-1708
    C. J-1939
    D. J-1996

57. Technician A says when combining batteries in a 12-volt parallel circuit, the voltage stays the same. Technician B says adding another battery in a 12-volt series circuit will double the voltage. Who is right?
    A. Technician A only
    B. Technician B only
    C. Both A and B
    D. Neither A or B

58. Technician A says to check for additional loads connected in parallel with a component being tested for resistance. Technician B says the power must be on in the circuit before checking resistance. Who is right?
    A. Technician A only
    B. Technician B only
    C. Both A and B
    D. Neither A or B

59. Another term for voltage drop is:
    A. potential equation
    B. potential difference
    C. variable voltage
    D. voltage cut

60. Technician A says a Digital Graphing Multimeter (GMM) can be used to view electronic waveforms. Technician B says GMMs can be used to view vehicle-specific information displayed on-screen. Who is right?
    A. Technician A only
    B. Technician B only
    C. Both A and B
    D. Neither A or B

61. Which of the following protects some starters from overheating while cranking?
    A. crank thermal switch
    B. circuit breaker
    C. crank lock switch
    D. crank limiting switch

62. Which of the following keeps the starter from being accidently engaged when the engine is running?
    A. cranking limiter system
    B. starter protection system
    C. starter key lockout system
    D. cranking inhibit system

Prepare yourself for ASE testing with these questions on MEDIUM/HEAVY ELECTRICAL/ELECTRONIC SYSTEMS

63. Technician A says if the alternator or voltage regulator draws current when the vehicle is off, there is a problem with parasitic draw. Technician B says computer memories and stored diagnostic data have no effect on parasitic draw. Who is right?
   A. Technician A
   B. Technician B
   C. Both A and B
   D. Neither A or B

64. Technician A says variable resistors change in accordance with temperature. Technician B says negative coefficient means a resistor raises its resistance as temperature rises. Who is right?
   A. Technician A
   B. Technician B
   C. Both A and B
   D. Neither A or B

65. Technician A says MAG system relays can be serviced on the vehicle. Technician B says IMS is integrated with the starter.
   A. Technician A
   B. Technician B
   C. Both A and B
   D. Neither A or B

Answers to Study-Guide Test Questions

1. The correct answer is B. A 12-volt test light is used to check for voltage. One lead must therefore be grounded before probing test points.

2. The correct answer is A. An ohmmeter, like a self-powered test light, can be used to check for continuity through a circuit. Since both have their own power sources, the circuits being tested must be un-powered. A plain 12-volt test light or multimeter set to volts is used to check for voltage already in the circuit.

3. The correct answer is D. There is voltage on one side of the switch. With the switch closed, there should be voltage at the other side as well. If not, the switch or its connector is not conducting current.

4. The correct answer is C. With the switch removed from the circuit, there is no way to check for voltage or current. A 12-volt test light, voltmeter and ammeter will not work. With the switch closed, continuity could be checked with a self-powered test light or ohmmeter.

5. The correct answer is C, both technicians are right. If there is voltage available at the bulb and it doesn't light, either the light isn't grounded or the bulb is burned out.

6. The correct answer is D. To check for continuity to ground, a self-powered test light or ohmmeter should be used between point I at the light bulb and point J or ground.

7. The correct answer is C. Either a short or a fuse of improper rating for the application will blow the fuse when the circuit is operated. In either case, there is too much current flow for the fuse to handle.

8. The correct answer is A. Since the fuse only blows when the switch is closed, the short must be in the switch, at the light bulb or in the wire between points G and H. If the short were before the switch, the new fuse would have blown the moment it was installed.

9. The correct answer is D, neither is right. The two most common types of circuit breakers are called thermal and magnetic. Thermal circuit breakers work by reaction to heat and cannot be manually reset. They must cool down to allow the bimetal strip to return to its normal position, closing the circuit. Magnetic circuit breakers use an electromagnet to trip the circuit breaker switch. Unlike the thermal circuit breaker, the magnetic circuit breaker can be manually reset.

10. The correct answer is C. Whenever a voltmeter is connected across two points where voltage should be present, it looks for the difference or drop in voltage between the two points.

11. The correct answer is A. Fiber optic cable is made up of thousands of tiny, flexible glass strands, which carry light reflections along the inner core of the cable. The inner core is wrapped by an outer core that helps to contain the light reflection.

12. The correct answer is D, neither technician is right. Under load, the voltage should be at least 9.6 volts, while the discharge rate should be three times the battery's amp-hour rating.

13. The correct answer is A. If high resistance before the light bulb were the problem, the test light would also be affected, and it, too, would glow dimly.

14. The correct answer is A. If there was a short to ground between the horn relay and the horn button, it would cause the relay to operate continuously, not make it fail to operate.

15. The correct answer is C, both technicians are right. Alternator noise can be caused by bad or dirty bearings, loose mountings, a defective diode or a shorted stator.

16. The correct answer is B. Using the equation, watts equals amps times volts, but solving for amps, we would multiply two times 50 watts and get 100 watts. Then, divide by 12 to get amps. The answer is about 8.3. A 10-amp fuse would be needed.

17. The correct answer is B. Batteries that are deeply discharged will freeze because the acid concentration decreases as the charge is used, leaving almost pure water.

18. The correct answer is A. When a new battery is teamed up with several older units, it will tend to carry a load greater than that for which it was designed. It will be doing part of the work that should be done by the other units, and therefore may fail prematurely. It is recommended to replace all the batteries.

19. The correct answer is B. A heavy truck alternator is typically sized to handle high accessory loads, and only a light charging load. Especially if there are high accessory loads after a jump start, the unit may very well be overloaded, causing it to overheat and fail.

Answers to Study-Guide Test Questions

20. The correct answer is B. The best charging voltage depends upon the time available for recharging and the degree to which batteries may become discharged during normal use. In such applications, a slightly higher charging voltage is appropriate and will not overcharge the batteries.

21. The correct answer is C. Some fiber optics use transducers to change electrical signals to light pulse signals. These light pulse signals are reflected along the fiber optic cable, and once they reach their destination, another transducer changes the light pulse back to an electrical signal.

22. The correct answer is A. Daytime running lights are usually illuminated at 50% or less of normal intensity. This is to distinguish them from the normal intensity of headlights..

23. The correct answer is C, both technicians are right. Loose alternator mounting bolts may prevent adequate belt tension, even if the primary adjusting bolt is tight. This leads to slippage and poor charging. Some alternators are grounded through their mounting bolts, and loose bolts may cause a poor ground and subsequent poor charging.

24. The correct answer is B. Charging problems may occasionally occur when the alternator would be adequate for the job with the engine turning near governed rpm, but spends much of the time operating down near the torque peak. An alternator with a different power curve will solve the problem.

25. The correct answer is B. Since the sending unit serves as ground for the warning light circuit, a ground elsewhere will cause the light to glow all the time.

26. The correct answer is A. Unless the weather is very cold, more than adequate starting performance will be supplied even when a battery is undercharged.

27. The correct answer is D. While cab mounts may possibly be used to carry current from cab accessories, they do not represent part of the starter ground circuit. The other three possibilities all represent critical parts of the starter ground circuit.

28. The correct answer is D. There are three basic voltage checks that should be made on the solenoid. First, test the voltage between the S terminal on the solenoid and ground. Next, test the voltage between the solenoid winding ground circuit G connector and ground. Finally, test the voltage drop between the solenoid B terminal and the terminal on top of the motor itself.

29. The correct answer is D. Although LEDs are visibly brighter than incandescent bulbs, they do not cast most of their light outward. Instead, the light is mostly confined within the bulb area, making the bulb itself more visible. LEDs also consume up to 90% less power than incandescent bulbs, helping to reduce the load on electrical systems and extend battery life. The only drawbacks to LED lighting are the initial price, and the fact that if a multiple light unit is subject to one or more bulb failures, the entire unit must be replaced. This is a rare occurrence, however, it does happen occasionally.

30. The correct answer is C, both technicians are right. If the vehicle is equipped with an inflatable Supplemental Restraint System (SRS) air bag, disarm the system according to manufacturer's procedures before servicing the horn button or wiring. Some horns are adjustable. Try to adjust the horns before replacing them. The adjusting screw is usually found on the horn body assembly. The adjustment screw should be set at the point where the horn current draw is between 4 and 6.5 amperes.

31. The correct answer is C, both technicians are right. The purpose of the low-pressure cutoff switch is compressor protection. The compressor clutch circuit is opened if the pressure in the system drops too low. This would be an indication that the system has lost some or all of its refrigerant charge. Since the lubricating oil is carried by the refrigerant, a loss could cause damage to the compressor if it were allowed to operate without sufficient lubrication.

32. The correct answer is D, neither is right. Using a metal work area can rob heat from the component to be soldered, which can make it difficult for the solder to melt. If possible, remove the component from the vehicle and place it on a wooden board. Soldering tips must be 'tinned' regularly for quick transfer of heat to the project and to prevent the solder from sticking to the iron. To tin the iron, heat it and touch the solder to the tip; the solder will flow over the hot tip. Wipe the excess off with a clean rag, using caution because the iron will be hot.

33. The correct answer is A. A starter should not be operated for more than 30 seconds continuously. The starter should be disengaged periodically to allow it to

Answers to Study-Guide Test Questions

cool. Overheating the starter by excessive cranking will severely damage the unit.

34. The correct answer is C. Contrary to popular belief, using an analog multimeter to test for resistance from the positive battery cable to ground, using the meter to test for a 12-volt draw, or using a test light in series with a battery cable is not the most accurate way to check for key-off battery drain. The most effective way of checking this condition is to use a digital multimeter, set to the amps mode, in series with a special test adapter. These adapters consist of a resistor pack, and are placed in series with the battery cable, and the DMM is connected to the test adapter to measure the voltage drop to determine the key-off drain measurement.

35. The correct answer is D. Since fluid sprays on one side of the windshield, the pump is working. The problem is most likely a kinked or blocked hose. If the fuse was blown or if there was no voltage to the pump, the pump would not operate at all. If the fluid level was low, it still would not affect which side of the windshield it was sprayed on.

36. The correct answer is C, both technicians are right. A hot electrical wire means more electrons are trying to flow through it than the wire is capable of carrying. Usually, this is a sign of trouble. Typically, that trouble would be either a deterioration of the wire, possibly due to a number of individual strands being broken in a conductor consisting of many individual strands, or higher-than-normal current flow due to a problem in the wiring or the load.

37. The correct answer is D, neither technician is right. A capacitor is a device that is used for holding or storing a surge of electrical current and releasing it as needed. It limits transient voltage across a circuit, thereby protecting components from damaging electrical surges. A diode is a device that controls the direction of electron flow. Generally, if one or two of the blower speeds don't work, the problem is a faulty resistor.

38. The correct answer is A. Insufficient cooling in the sleeper can be the result of an inoperative solenoid valve. The function of the ambient temperature sensor is to inhibit compressor clutch operation in cold ambient temperatures. If the solar sensor was defective, air would be the same temperature at all outlets. If the refrigerant was low, warm air would come out of all vents, not just the sleeper vents.

39. The correct answer is D. For maximum protection to the computer controlled systems or any solid-state circuit, you should use at least a 10-megohm impedance DMM.

40. The correct answer is C, both technicians are right. A short to ground has little or no resistance. Current flow increases as resistance decreases.

41. The correct answer is A. The high-pressure cutoff switch interrupts voltage to the compressor in the event of high system pressures. This is to protect the system, and also to prevent the venting of refrigerant.

42. The correct answer is C. Resistance is measured using the ohms setting. Resistance is the opposition offered by a component to steady electric current passing through.

43. The correct answer is C, both technicians are right. ECM trouble codes that are stored in memory are removable by either selecting an option on the diagnostic reader, or on some older models, disrupting the power source to the ECM for a short period of time. Of course, there is a distinct disadvantage to the latter procedure. If the codes are removed by someone, all history of the electronic malfunctions stored in the ECM are also removed.

44. The correct answer is D. Some high-rate discharge testers will test a battery as low as 25% charged by adjusting a percent-of-charge switch. Since hydrometer readings indicate only the chemical condition, the battery should be subjected to a high-rate discharge (or load) test to determine its ability to deliver current under load.

45. The correct answer is A. The green and yellow wires in the light cord plug supply current to the trailer turn signals. If the tractor fuse that operates the turn signals was blown, the signals on the tractor would also not work.

46. The correct answer is C, both technicians are right. According to U.S. Department of Transportation Federal Highway Administration (FHWA) Motor Carrier Safety Regulations, the battery or batteries, unless located in the engine compartment, must be covered by a fixed part of the vehicle, or a removable cover.

Answers to Study-Guide Test Questions

47. The correct answer is C. The function of the alternator/voltage regulator is to keep the system voltage within a predetermined range, typically 13.5-14.5 volts.

48. The correct answer is A. Manual transmission models employ a clutch switch that opens and disengages the cruise control circuit when the clutch pedal is depressed. When the pedal is released, the system will stay disengaged.

49. The correct answer is D. Any additional resistance that is not supposed to be in a circuit can cause a voltage drop in that circuit. This means there will be less available voltage flowing in the circuit to perform its function. Voltage drops are usually caused by poor connections, such as corrosion in connectors, faulty solder joints, paint between a wiring connector and firewall, and so on.

50. The correct answer is C. The battery and other electrical accessories in the electrical system operate on Direct Current (DC), which flows in one direction only. For this reason it is necessary to change AC to DC. This function is performed by rectifying diodes.

51. The correct answer is A. If there is AC voltage at the back of the outlet, but no voltage from the outlet socket, suspect a defective outlet. If DC voltage exists at the inverter input and there is no AC voltage coming from the inverter, suspect a problem with the inverter itself. In this case, none of the accessories would be operative.

52. The correct answer is C. The technician should check the battery charge first. The LVD unit monitors battery voltage and disconnects the load when voltage is below normal. If voltage falls below specifications, the load is automatically disconnected, saving the batteries from complete discharge. When battery charging is restored, the load is automatically reconnected.

53. The correct answer is D, neither technician is right. Only some dashboards use a voltage regulator to supply a constant 3 volts to all the dash gauges. In cases where all the gauges develop similar problems all at the same time, the voltage regulator is at fault.

54. The correct answer is D. LEDs can remain effective for up to 100,000 hours, while their incandescent counterparts may remain effective from 200 to 15,000 hours, depending upon the size of the bulb and conditions in which the bulb is exposed.

55. The correct answer is D. A remote sensing alternator improves upon charging by recognizing actual load need instead of charging at a standard alternator output. This type of alternator bases its output on such variables as required voltage and ambient temperature.

56. The correct answer is C. The most recent data bus system used by heavy-truck manufacturers is designated J-1939. The network widely in use today is called a Controlled Area Network (CAN). This is a high-speed engineering standard that is designed to allow computers to transmit information via the vehicle's J-1939 data bus.

57. The correct answer is C, both technicians are right. Two 12-volt batteries wired in parallel will still yield 12 volts. Multiple batteries are often connected in parallel in heavy-duty truck applications. When combining batteries in a series circuit, double the voltage is obtained. For example, two 12-volt batteries in series produce a large 24-volt battery.

58. The correct answer is A. When checking the resistance of a load, make sure there is not another resistor or other component connected in parallel with the component being tested. Such a unit would have to be disconnected in order for you to get an accurate reading. To measure resistance, turn the power off in the circuit before connecting the meter.

59. The correct answer is B. Voltage drop can be termed as the potential or potential difference that designates electric pressure between two or more points.

60. The correct answer is C, both technicians are right. GMMs recognize the difference between normal and unusual signal patterns, with the capability of saving and storing data for analysis and repair. They translate an electronic signal into a waveform and display it on screen. Most GMMs have a database that holds vehicle-specific information.

61. The correct answer is B. Some starters are equipped with a circuit breaker that trips when the starter overheats due to over cranking. This is called over crank protection (OCP). Over crank protection ensures that the starter motor only operates under its normal working temperature. The circuit breaker will reset once the starter reaches a normal specified operating temperature.

Answers to Study-Guide Test Questions

62. The correct answer is D. Some trucks are equipped with a cranking inhibit system that keeps the starter from being accidentally cranked when the engine is running. This helps to reduce damage to the flywheel and starter drive gear.

63. The correct answer is B. The alternator and voltage regulator draw very small amounts of current while the vehicle is off. This is not a problem for today's vehicles as long as the drain is not excessive. Components such as computer memories and stored diagnostic data must be kept whether the vehicle is running or not. In most cases, there will be a very slight draw on the battery because of computerized systems in the vehicle that need voltage at all times in order to function properly.

64. The correct answer is D, neither technician. Variable resistors have a sliding contact so the amount of resistance can be changed. Another resistor, called a thermistor, changes in accordance with temperature. A negative coefficient means the thermistor lowers its resistance as temperature rises.

65. The correct answer is B, both technicians. Some magnetic relays are located in the engine compartment and some are integrated with the starter assembly. If the magnetic relay is integrated with the starter, the system is called an Integrated MAG system, or IMS.

Glossary of Terms

--a--

actuator - control device that delivers mechanical action in response to a vacuum or electrical signal; anything that the engine control computer uses to do something, such as trigger fuel injection or fire a spark plug. Most actuators on a computer-controlled engine system are activated by grounding their circuits rather than by actively powering them, since that protects the computer from short circuits.

aftermarket - parts and equipment manufacturing that is not original equipment from the factory.

air bag (SRS) - actuated component of the supplemental restraint system, developed for safety.

alternating current (AC) - an electrical current that moves first in one direction and then in the other (positive to negative then negative to positive).

alternator - an AC generator that produces alternating current, which is internally rectified to DC current before being released.

ambient temperature - the temperature of the air surrounding an object.

American Trucking Associations (ATA) - organization formed to advance the trucking industry's image, efficiency, competitiveness and profitability; to provide educational programs and industry research; and to promote highway and driver safety.

ammeter - an instrument used to measure the rate of current flow in a circuit.

amperage - the total amount of current (amperes) flowing in a circuit.

ampere (amp) - a unit of measurement for the flow of electrical current in a circuit.

amplifier - a circuit or device used to increase the voltage or current of a signal.

amplify - to enlarge or strengthen original characteristics; usually used in reference to electronics.

analog - a non-digital measuring method that uses a needle to indicate readings.

analog multimeter - non-digital measuring method that uses a needle to indicate readings. Analog meters should not be used on solid-state electronics.

analog processing - method of processing information used in older ABS control units. Today's Electronic Control Units (ECUs) use digital processing, which is many times faster and more reliable.

armature - internal rotating component of an electric motor that converts electrical current into mechanical energy. An armature is comprised of a soft iron core and wrapped with wire. Starters, generators and compressor clutches have armatures.

ASE - see National Institute for Automotive Service Excellence.

ATA - see American Trucking Associations.

--b--

ballast resistor - resistor in the primary side of the ignition system that is used to reduce voltage by approximately 4-5 volts.

battery - a device used to store electrical energy in a chemical form.

battery acid - sulfuric acid solution used as the electrolyte in a battery.

battery cell - the part of a storage battery made from two dissimilar metals and an acid solution. A cell stores chemical energy to be used later as electrical energy.

blower motor - electric motor that drives the fan, which circulates air inside the vehicle passenger compartment.

bobtail - tractor that runs without a trailer.

brush - a piece of conducting material that, when bearing against a commutator, slip ring, etc., will provide a passage for electric current.

--c--

cab over engine (COE) - vehicle that has its cab mounted directly over the engine compartment. Because the COE truck has greater maneuverability, it is mostly used in urban areas where a smaller turning radius is required.

Glossary of Terms

capacitor (condenser) - a device used to store an electrical charge.

capacity - the quantity of electricity that can be delivered from a unit, as from a battery in ampere hours, or output from a generator, etc.

carbon pile - a device to vary the resistance and, consequently, the current in an electrical circuit.

charge - electrical current that passes through the battery to restore it to full power; to fill, or bring up to the specific level, an A/C system with refrigerant; the required amount of refrigerant for an A/C system.

charging system - system that supplies electrical power for vehicle operation and recharges the battery.

circuit (closed) - an electrical circuit in which there is no interruption of current flow.

circuit (open) - any break or lack of contact in an electrical circuit either intentional (switch) or unintentional (bad connection).

circuit (parallel) - an electrical system in which all positive terminals are joined through one wire, and all negative terminals through another wire.

circuit (series) - an electrical system in which separate parts are connected end-to-end, to form a single path for current to flow through.

circuit (series parallel) - the connection of several loads in a circuit in such a way that current must flow through some loads, but can flow to one or more of the other loads without affecting the rest of the circuit. A series parallel circuit is simply a circuit containing elements of both a series circuit and a parallel circuit.

circuit breaker - uses a heat-sensitive spring to break contact in an overload condition. Automotive circuit breakers will reset to close the circuit when they cool off.

circuit protector - a circuit protector is a device that will open the circuit if it becomes overheated because of too much electricity flowing through it. Thus it protects other components from damage if the circuit is accidentally grounded or overloaded. Fuses, fusible links and circuit breakers are circuit protectors.

closed circuit - an electrical circuit in which there is no interruption of current flow.

coil - a continuous winding arrangement of a conductor that combines the separate magnetic fields of all the winding loops to produce a single, stronger field.

cold cranking amps (CCA) - a battery rating system, which is the number of amps, a battery can deliver for 30 seconds at 0°F (at 1.2 volts per cell).

commutator - slotted ring located at the end of the armature of a generator or motor. The commutator provides the electrical connection between the armature and brushes.

condenser (capacitor) - a device for holding or storing an electrical charge.

conductors - cables and wires used to conduct electricity between components. They are normally made up of several strands of copper, covered with insulation. The insulation comes in various colors to provide coding for the wires and to make it easier to trace circuits. Wires are frequently gathered and wrapped together into harnesses.

cranking inhibit system - system that keeps the starter from being accidentally cranked when the engine is running. This helps to reduce damage to the flywheel and starter drive gear.

current - the flow of electricity in a circuit.

--d--

data link connector - means through which information about the state of the vehicle control system can be extracted with a scan tool. This information includes actual readouts on each sensor's input circuit and some actuator signals. It also includes any trouble codes stored.

daytime running lights (DRL) - headlights are illuminated at 50% or less of normal intensity when the ignition switch is turned ON.

Department Of Transportation (DOT) - bureau established to assure the coordinated, effective administration of transportation programs and to develop national standardized transportation policies.

diagnostic flow chart - usually found in OEM service manuals, a diagnostic flow chart is a diagram that gives a step-by-step approach to diagnosing a malfunction in a vehicle.

Glossary of Terms

diagnostic trouble code (DTC) - code that represents and can be used to identify a malfunction in a computer control system.

digital - a voltage signal that uses on and off pulses.

digital multimeter (DMM) - instrument that measures volts, ohms and amps and displays the results numerically.

digital volt/ohmmeter (DVOM) - see digital multimeter (DMM).

diode - a device that permits current to flow in one direction only. Used to change alternating current to direct current. A rectifier.

direct current (DC) - an electrical current that flows in one direction only.

direction of current flow - current flows through a circuit from the positive terminal of the source to the negative terminal.

draw (amperage) - the amount of current required to operate an electrical device.

driveability - degree to which a vehicle operates properly, including starting, running smoothly, accelerating and delivering reasonable fuel mileage.

drop (voltage) - the net difference in electrical pressure when measured on both sides of a resistance.

dropping resistor - device that reduces battery voltage in a circuit.

--e--

ECM - see electronic control module.

electric transfer pump - its purpose is to move the fuel from the storage tank, through a strainer and fuel filter to the rest of the system at low pressure.

electrolyte - a material whose atoms become ionized (electrically charged) in solution. The battery electrolyte is a mixture of sulfuric acid and water.

electromagnet - a coil that produces a magnetic field when current flows through its windings.

electromagnetic induction - the principle by which an alternator converts mechanical energy into electrical energy. The rotating magnetic field carried by the field coils in a generator cuts through stator windings linked to a load. When that happens, current is generated on the stator windings, and the torque required to turn the rotor, which carries the field, is increased.

electromechanical - refers to a device that incorporates both electrical and mechanical principles together in its operation.

electromotive force - the force or pressure that causes current movement in an electrical circuit.

electronic - pertaining to the control of systems or devices by the use of small electrical signals and various semiconductors.

electronically programmable memory (EPROM) - memory chip that allows an ECM to adapt to certain vehicle functions.

electronic control module (ECM) - a microprocessor that is powered by the electrical system. It reads various engine parameters such as crankshaft position, rpm, boost pressure, throttle position, etc.

emitter - a portion of a transistor from which electrons are emitted or forced out.

EPROM - see electronically programmable memory.

--f--

Federal Highway Administration (FHWA) - Department of Transportation (DOT) agency that administers federal highway funding and implements regulations, policies and guidelines for safety, access and development of U.S. highways.

Federal Motor Carrier Safety Administration (FMCSA) - Department of Transportation (DOT) agency that establishes and enforces safety regulations regarding commercial motor vehicles.

Federal Motor Vehicle Safety Standards (FMVSS) - Department of Transportation (DOT) standards a vehicle must meet before it is produced for the consumer.

fiber optics - thousands of tiny, flexible glass strands wrapped by an outer core, which carry light reflections along the inner core of a cable.

Glossary of Terms

field (magnetic) - the area in which magnetic lines of force occur.

field coil - a wire coil on an alternator rotor or starter motor frame; a field coil produces a magnetic field when energized.

field current - a small amount of battery current allowed to flow through the alternator's rotor windings, forming the magnetic field that causes the alternator to generate current.

filament - a high-resistance wire in a light bulb that glows and produces light when a current is forced through it.

flux density - degree of concentration of the magnetic lines of force that emanate from a magnetic sensor; when the tooth of a reluctor aligns with the sensor tip, the magnetic lines of force are squeezed together, which increases flux density.

fuse - a plug-in protector with a filament that melts or burns out when overloaded.

fusible link - a wire section with fewer strands of wire than the rest of the circuit. It melts or burns out if overloaded.

--g--

Gross Combination Weight (GCW) - total weight of a combination vehicle including the driver, fuel and payload.

Gross Trailer Weight (GTW) - total weight of a trailer along with its payload.

Gross Vehicle Weight (GVW) - total weight of a vehicle along with its payload.

ground - the end point for current. Generally the negative pole of the battery.

growler - a device for testing an electric motor or generator armature.

GTW - see gross trailer weight.

GVW - see gross vehicle weight.

--h--

halogen light - light that is contained in a pressurized gas environment, which allows the filament to be heated to higher temperatures. This produces a much brighter and whiter light, requiring less power than normal sealed beams.

heat sink - device to dissipate heat and protect components.

hydrometer - an instrument with a float housed in a glass tube that measures the specific gravity of a liquid.

--i--

ignition coil - transforms the low 12-volt battery ignition primary current into the high voltage secondary current that fires the spark in the plugs. The current through the primary coil windings builds up an electromagnetic field around the ferrous core of the coil. When the current is suddenly shut off, the electromagnetic field collapses and generates the high voltage in the secondary windings.

ignition delay - length of time or number of degrees of crankshaft rotation between the beginning of injection and ignition of the fuel.

ignition switch - key operated switch located on the steering column, which connects and disconnects power to the ignition and electrical systems.

ignition system - components that produce the spark to ignite the air/fuel mixture in the combustion chamber.

impedance - total resistance of an electrical device measured in ohms.

inductance - the force that produces voltage when a conductor is passed through a magnetic field.

insulator - a non-conducting substance or body, such as porcelain, glass or Bakelite, used for insulating wires in electrical circuits to prevent the undesired flow of electricity.

integrated circuit - electrical circuit containing many interconnected amplifying devices and circuit elements formed on a single body or chip of semiconductor material; diodes, transistors and other electronic components mounted on semiconductor material and able to perform numerous functions.

Glossary of Terms

integrated MAG system (IMS) - magnetic relay integrated with the starter assembly. If the magnetic relay is integrated with the starter, the system is called an Integrated MAG system, or IMS.

--k--

keep-alive memory - series of vehicle battery-powered memory locations in the microcomputer that store information on input failure, identified in normal operations for use in diagnostic routines; adapts some calibration parameters to compensate for changes in the vehicle system.

--l--

light-emitting diode (LED) - a type of digital electronic display used as either single or grouped indicators.

liquid crystal diode (LCD) - type of digital electronic display made of special glass and liquid; requires a separate light source.

load - an electrical device that harnesses moving electrons and puts them to work.

low voltage disconnect system - separates the load from the battery if battery voltage falls below manufacturer's specifications. This helps to prevent battery deep cycling.

--m--

magnet - any substance that attracts iron or an iron, steel or any ferrous metal alloy.

magnetic field - the areas surrounding the poles of a magnet that are affected by its forces of attraction or repulsion.

malfunction indicator light (MIL) - also known as the CHECK ENGINE or SERVICE ENGINE SOON light on many vehicles. The MIL comes on when the ignition is first turned on to check the bulb and perform a system check, and then goes out once the engine is started, unless a trouble code is stored in the computer. If the MIL is on when the vehicle is running, there has been a malfunction on one of the sensor or actuator circuits monitored by the computer, and a diagnosis will have to be made by retrieving the code.

memory - part of a computer that stores or holds programs and other data.

meter - instrument used for measuring, especially the flow of a gas, liquid or electrical charge; to regulate the flow of a gas, liquid or electrical charge; to control the amount of fuel passing into an injector or carburetor.

microprocessor - the portion of a microcomputer that receives sensor input and handles calculations.

module - electronic control unit.

motor - an electro-magnetic device used to convert electrical energy into mechanical energy.

multiplexing - a means of using a single circuit to carry a number of gauge signals to a number of individual dashboard gauges. Each gauge is programmed to read only the signal applied to it. Thus, wiring and diagnosis are greatly simplified.

--n--

National Institute for Automotive Service Excellence (ASE, formerly NIASE) - nonprofit certification agency for automotive, truck, school bus, auto body, engine machine shop and parts personnel.

National Highway Traffic Safety Administration (NHTSA) - Department of Transportation (DOT) agency established to carry out safety programs. NHTSA investigates safety defects in motor vehicles, sets and enforces fuel economy standards, helps states and local communities reduce the threat of drunk drivers, promotes the use of safety belts, child safety seats and air bags, investigates odometer fraud, establishes and enforces vehicle anti-theft regulations and provides consumer information on motor vehicle safety topics.

negative temperature coefficient thermistor - thermistor that loses electrical resistance as it gets warmer. The temperature sensors for the computer control system are negative temperature coefficient thermistors. The effect is to systematically lower the 5-volt reference voltage sent them by the computer, yielding a signal that corresponds to the temperature of the measured source.

neutral start switch - switch that prevents starter engagement if the transmission is in another gear besides Park or Neutral.

Glossary of Terms

NHTSA - see National Highway Traffic Safety Administration.

--o--

OEM - acronym for Original Equipment Manufacturer.

ohm - a unit of measurement of electrical resistance.

ohmmeter - instrument that measures electrical resistance in ohms.

ohm's law - a law of electricity, which states the relationship between voltage, amperes and resistance. It takes a pressure of one volt to force one ampere of current through one ohm of resistance. Equation: Volts = amperes × ohms (E=I×R).

open circuit - any break or lack of contact in an electrical circuit, either intentional (switch) or unintentional (bad connection).

oscilloscope - instrument that displays electrical activity in the form of line patterns on a screen.

over crank protection (OCP) - starter that is equipped with an integrated circuit breaker that trips, cutting voltage to the relay when the starter is excessively overheated.

--p--

parallel circuit - an electrical system in which all positive terminals are joined through one wire, and all negative terminals through another wire.

parasitic draw - current draw on a vehicle electrical system when the vehicle is not running and an electrical circuit is operating when it is not supposed to operate.

piezoelectric sensor - sensor that generates voltage from physical shock or motion, a knock sensor.

polarity - the condition of being polar. That is, having a positive and a negative.

printed circuit - electrical circuit formed by electrically conductive paths printed on a board.

Programmable Read Only Memory (PROM) - memory chip that contains specific information pertaining to a certain vehicle model.

pulse width - length of time during which a circuit is energized.

pulse width modulated - electronic control of a solenoid that rapidly cycles it on and off many times per second in order to achieve a specific output.

--r--

random access memory (RAM) - type of memory used in a computer to store information temporarily.

read-only memory (ROM) - type of memory used in a computer to store information permanently, as opposed to the temporary storage provided by random-access memory (RAM).

rectifier - an electrical device containing diodes, used to convert AC to DC.

rectify - to change one type of voltage to another.

reference pulse - voltage signal generated by the crankshaft position sensor (or distributor, or camshaft position sensor — all equivalent components for this purpose). The voltage signal is sent to the computer as a fixed number of degrees BTDC for each cylinder, with the signal for cylinder No. 1 distinguishable from the signal for the others.

reference voltage - voltage supplied by the system computer to certain sensors. The sensors reduce the voltage by a specific amount, according to their function, and send the signal back to the computer. The computer then uses the reduced voltage signal to interpret the information sent.

relay - an electro-magnetic switching device using low current to open or close a high-current circuit.

remote sense - monitors small voltage drops as the voltage travels from the alternator to the battery. If a small voltage drop is detected, the alternator will boost the voltage to compensate. This helps to prolong battery life.

reserve capacity - the number of minutes a battery can deliver 25 amps at 80°F (1.75 volts per cell).

resistance - that property of an electrical circuit that prevents or reduces the flow of current.

Glossary of Terms

resistor - a device installed in an electrical circuit to permit a predetermined current to flow with a given voltage applied.

rheostat - a device for regulating a current by means of a variable resistance.

rotor - the part of the alternator that rotates inside the stator and produces an electrical current from induction by the electro-magnetic fields of the stator windings.

--s--

SAE - see Society of Automotive Engineers.

scan tool - microprocessor designed to communicate with the vehicle's onboard computer system to perform diagnostic and troubleshooting functions.

scan tool data - information from the vehicle computer that is displayed on the scan tool. This data includes component and system values on the data stream, DTCs, and on some systems, freeze frame data, system monitors and readiness monitors.

semiconductor - material that is neither a good conductor of electricity nor a good insulator.

sensor - any mechanism by which the engine control computer can measure some variable on the engine, such as coolant temperature or engine speed. Each sensor works by sending the computer a signal of some sort, a coded electronic message that corresponds to some point on the range of the variable measured by that sensor.

series circuit - an electrical system in which separate parts are connected end-to-end, to form a single path through which current can flow.

series-parallel circuit - the connection of several loads in a circuit in such a way that current must flow through some loads, but can flow to one or more of the other loads without affecting the rest of the circuit. A series-parallel circuit is simply a circuit containing elements of both a series circuit and a parallel circuit.

short circuit - condition that occurs in an electrical circuit when the current bypasses the intended load and takes a path with little or no resistance, such as another circuit or ground.

shunt - a conductor joining two points in a circuit to form a parallel circuit, through which a portion of the current may pass, in order to regulate the amount of current flowing in the main circuit.

solenoid - an electromagnetic switch that converts an electrical signal into mechanical operation.

solid state - electrical device with no moving parts.

specific gravity - the ratio of sulfuric acid to water in a battery. The resulting solution is heavier than water; its density is measured with a hydrometer.

square wave/sine wave - voltage fluctuations of different shapes in an electric circuit. The square wave goes immediately from one voltage to the other; the sine wave gradually changes, going through the intervening values. An electromagnetic pulse generator like a wheel speed sensor or a reluctor-type distributor pickup produces a sine wave. Hall Effect sensors, photoelectric switches, and other on-off signal generators produce square waves.

stator - the stationary winding of an alternator (the armature in a DC generator).

switch - a device used to open, close or redirect current in an electrical circuit.

--t--

Technology and Maintenance Council (TMC) - formerly named The Maintenance Council. Branch of the American Trucking Associations dedicated to providing technology solutions to the trucking industry through education, networking, and standards development.

terminal - a device attached to the end of a wire, cable or load to make an electrical connection.

thermal limiter - component similar to a fuse, which blows to open the compressor clutch circuit when the superheat switch detects low system pressure.

three-phase alternating current - a combination of three independent currents generated by the three phases of the alternator stator windings. The current in each of the three phases rises and falls at different times, in such a way as to make the total output current almost perfectly steady.

TMC - see Technology and Maintenance Council.

Glossary of Terms

Truck Trailer Manufacturers Association (TTMA) - agency that establishes and maintains relationships between manufacturers of truck trailers, cargo tanks, intermodal containers and their suppliers.

--v--

Vehicle Identification Number (VIN) - combination of numbers and letters unique to each vehicle that identifies certain characteristics of the vehicle.

vehicle speed sensor (VSS) - permanent magnet sensor, usually located on the transmission, which provides an input to the vehicle computer control system regarding vehicle speed.

volt - unit of electromotive force. One volt of electromotive force applied steadily to a conductor of one-ohm resistance produces a current of one ampere.

voltage - electrical pressure that causes current flow in a circuit.

voltage drop - voltage lost by the passage of electrical current through resistance.

voltage regulator - device used to control the output of an alternator or generator.

voltmeter - instrument used to measure voltage in a circuit.

--w--

watt - the unit for measuring electrical power or work. A watt is the mathematical product of amperes and volts (W=A×V).

--z--

zener diode - silicone diode that allows current to flow in the opposite direction, once an applied voltage reaches a certain level.

Glossary of Terms